The Easiest Way to Live

by Mabel Katz

Your Business Press

The Easiest Way to Live

*Let go of the past, live in the present
and change your life forever*

by Mabel Katz
Preface by Dr. Ihaleakalá Hew Len

Publisher's Cataloging-in-Publication
Katz, Mabel
The Easiest Way to Live: Let go of the past, live in the present and change your life
forever / Mabel Katz - 1st ed. pbk. p.cm.

LCCN TXu1-675-769   **ISBN** 978-0-9825910-4-8

1. Self realization   **2.** Control (Psychology)
3. Problem solving

The Easiest Way to Live
Copyright © 2010 Mabel Katz

Cover Photo and Design: Erika Aguilar
Book Design: Eduardo Venegas
Editors: Diana Valori, Deborah Barnet, Mirta J. Atlas

Your Business Press

PO Box 427
Woodland Hills, CA 91365
(818) 668-2085
support@mabelkatz.com
www.BusinessByYou.com

PRINTED IN THE UNITED STATES OF AMERICA

The Easiest Way to Live

Let go of the past, live in the present and change your life forever

Dedication

I dedicate this book to everybody in
search for happiness, peace and an easier
way to live.

Acknowledgments

I wish to express my gratitude to the following:

To God, for all the blessings he has bestowed upon me, and the abundant trust He placed in me as I journey to share the inspirations and the answers He deposits into my heart.

To my mother, who has always been there with her love and support no matter what.

To my two wonderful sons, Jonathan & Lyonel for their love, support and understanding of my journey. Thank you both for being part of my life and my mission.

To Yael Baruch, for her encouragement and the push I needed that helped me to finally sit and find the time and the inspiration to write this book.

To Dr. Ihaleakalá Hew Len, for what I have learned from him has given me such spiritual growth and strength. I am a blessed and better person today because of his influence throughout my journey.

To Morrnah Simeona, for her devoted teachings and inspirations.

To my dedicated editors and friends, Mirta J. Atlas, Deborah Barnet and Diana Valori for believing in me and this book and for the many hours of dedication and support.

To my students all over the world, and their wonderful testimonies that gave me the convictions I needed to continue this work and the confidence and strength to keep going.

Thank you. Thank you very much.

Preface

In *The Easiest Way to Live*, Mabel (Kikiko'ele) shares insights on "the easiest way to live." I got the following from her book:

1. I am GOD-MADE, created by Divine Love in its exact likeness, "pure in heart";
2. My ONLY PURPOSE in life is to be myself, "pure in heart";
3. My ONLY TASK in life is to release memories – errors – replaying problems in my subconscious from my past that block me from being myself, "pure in heart";
4. By applying the ancient HO'OPONOPONO problem solving process, I can petition Divinity to restore me to my original state of "purity of heart" by releasing my memories to zero;

5. I am 100% RESPONSIBLE for creating the memories stored in my subconscious mind that I re-experience as problems;
6. Moment by moment, I have a CHOICE to restore my original state of "purity of heart" by applying the ancient Ho'oponopono problem solving process ceaselessly, moment by moment, and
7. No problems exist outside of me. My problems exist only in me as MEMORIES REPLAYING in my subconscious mind.

Our only purpose for existence is to restore our original state of "purity of heart" by freeing ourselves from memories replaying problems from the past in our subconscious mind.

"Love your enemies," a great sage said more than two thousand years ago. Our enemies are our memories replaying fear, anger, resentment, hate, attachments and judgment from the past. We can take 100% responsibility for them by applying easy to use ancient Ho'oponopono problem solving processes such as "I love you" and "Thank you."

I highly recommend *The Easiest Way to Live* by Mabel Katz

POI
Dr. Ihaleakalá Hew Len

Introduction

After I presented my first classes in Israel, in June 2009, Yael, my publisher in that country, came up to me and said, "Mabel, your book *The Easiest Way* is great, and you must write another one. That book was Mabel in 2003, not the Mabel of today. You have come a long way and have so much more to share."

Sharing and making a difference is what I love to do, so I thought for a minute and then said, "YES." You see, I had been thinking about writing this new book for many years but I was procrastinating.

Around this same time I was receiving messages from people in different parts of the world saying, "You must sit down and write it yourself, as you did with your first book, coming from pure Inspiration." I couldn't just record and ask somebody else to help transcribe my words, nor use a ghost writer, because the inspiration had to come through me.

Well, let me tell you that, once I made up my mind, a lot of Inspiration came my way. That wonderful Inspiration and the many life experiences I had in the process helped me become more present and aware and allowed me to finally make this book a reality.

I would like to begin by sharing that, when my kids were still little, I would tell them that their job was to be happy; that happy people were "lucky." I don't think I actually knew what I was talking about at that time.

Maybe now I can explain it a little better.
You are lucky when you are happy, because you become an open channel, and as an open channel,

you allow the part of you that created you and knows you better than anyone else to guide you. The dance of the Universe will always put you in the right place at the right time when you open your channels to give permission.

When you believe in yourself and accept life just the way it is, when you realize that every problem in your life is a step toward your freedom and that you don't need to be right and/or have the last word, you automatically feel lighter and happier.

Good luck means to be in the right place, at the right time, with the right people. Usually you are lucky when you get out of your own way. As you stop the chattering in your head and open your heart, you allow miracles to come your way.

All you have to do is trust in your heart. The secrets to finding your joy, happiness, inner peace and freedom are hidden in your heart.

The concepts and messages in this book are merely reminders that you are the only one who can change your life. There is no one out there doing anything to you, and you are responsible (not guilty) for the people and situations you attract to your life. This book seeks to remind you that the light and love you so long for are behind every challenge in your life and that the more challenges you face, the more blessings you will receive.

Our ancestors knew that the solutions to our problems could only come from heaven, so they were moved by trust and faith, which allowed them to see and experience amazing miracles. They knew that miracles happened every time they decided to let go of thinking and gave permission for the perfect solution to show up, even without knowing where it was going to come from.

This book contains a number of different chapters and themes to help you be more conscious. They concentrate on the following main ideas:
- There is no one out there, just you and your thoughts.
- You are 100% responsible, not guilty.
- When a door closes, another one opens automatically.
- The light is hidden behind every challenge in your life.

- Only you can set yourself free, especially from yourself!
- More opposition equals more blessings.
- When you change, everything changes.
- Peace starts with you.

In 2003, I wrote *The Easiest Way* because I had to share the secret of my discoveries, the things that changed my life. I needed to share this with everyone: "We all have the power to change our lives without depending on anyone or anything outside ourselves."

And now my passion and mission are to wake you up, so you can change your life and find the Peace, Happiness and Freedom I have found and know you are seeking.

I was so sure of what I discovered as I witnessed these concepts change so many lives, that I let go of my very profitable career as an accountant to travel the world sharing this message.

For some of you this book may be a reminder, for others it will be a confirmation. Whatever the case, I have no doubt that, if you are willing to open up, be flexible, and let go of the part of you that thinks it knows, you will find your answers. Just be aware that sometimes your mind will do anything to be right. My question to you is: Do you want to be right or happy?

If there is something in your life that is not working the way you would like it to work, if you are not happy or at peace, I am going to ask you to just send your intellect on a walk and read this book with your heart.

I sincerely hope you choose *The Easiest Way to Live*.

Chapter I

You Are Perfect

Who am I? That is the most important question, and most of us have no idea how simple its answer is.

It is important to remember that we all came from the Void, and this Perfect Light created us "Perfect," as something that is perfect cannot create anything imperfect. Perfect means no opinions, no beliefs, and no judgments.

We are perfect! However, thoughts, beliefs, opinions, and judgments are imperfect. These confusing and limiting programs and memories are inserted in our awareness by society and our experiences throughout our lifetimes.

When we become aware that we are not our memories, we can start observing without being attached to the outcome and return to our original state of perfection.

Simply observe your reaction to people and situations without engaging or reacting. As you master this process, you will become more aware of your thoughts, opinions, and judgments and be able to distance yourself from them and remain at peace in every situation. When you become able to observe without labeling a situation as good or bad, you set yourself free.

Unfortunately, our normal way of operating is to wait until we have certain situations arise before we decide, act or feel. We "become" according to external circumstances and believe this is who we are. Thus, we allow possessions, circumstances and external input to define our identity.

In order to recover our connection with the Divine and our inner peace, we must return to our real essence and know in our heart that we already have everything. This allows us to be ourselves and begin existing in a place of trust and inspiration, which in turn brings all that is perfect for us at each moment.

In almost every instance, you will receive more than you ever imagined when you stop defining yourself according to your external circumstances. Once you return to your true essence, people will appreciate you more because you appreciate yourself. Others will recognize you for your love and respect to yourself and your confidence. Their acknowledgment will have nothing to do with your degrees or what you have, and everything to do with YOU. This process is simple and natural. As soon as you begin to set yourself free, you will notice you don't need to say much for people to start asking, "What have you done to yourself? What have you been doing? You look different, younger!"

Marianne Williamson has said, "Our deepest fear is not that we are inadequate. Our deepest fear is that we are powerful beyond measure. It is our light, not our darkness that most frightens us. We ask ourselves, 'Who am I to be brilliant, gorgeous, talented, and fabulous?' Actually, who are you not to be? You are a child of God. Your playing small does not serve the world. There is nothing enlightened about shrinking so that other people won't feel insecure around you. We are all meant to shine, as children do. We were born to make manifest the glory of God that is within us. It's not just in some of us; it's in everyone. And as we let our own light shine, we unconsciously give other people permission to do the same. As we are liberated from our own fear, our presence automatically liberates others."

When you are yourself, you allow others to be themselves in your presence.

It might seem difficult at first, but once you have had this experience of awareness, which is being at zero (no opinions, judgments or expectations), you will want to go back there as often as possible, even for a split second. And the more you practice, the easier it will be to stay conscious. You may stay aware for a short time because the next memory will begin playing, thus giving you another opportunity to practice awareness and being yourself.

More and more, you will feel free like a little child who observes and admires the wonder of life. You will become "pure of heart." And at a certain point, it will require more effort to go back to the unaware life than the other way around. Being aware and being YOU are easy. It is natural, and once you start practicing, you will remember the feeling in your heart and body. The feeling will come back to you more and more. This state of peace and true joy is achieved moment by moment, letting go of whatever is not you.

Remember, the security and happiness you are seeking is not in your material possessions, your degrees, or relationships. It is much closer than you think.

Nothing, absolutely nothing external can make you feel complete or perfect. Everything you find on the outside, that you may now consider necessary, only gives you a temporary thrill. It is an attachment, and sooner or later, it might go away, or you might lose interest, and you may suffer.

Set yourself free. Realize you already have everything you need and don't need anything else. Let go and allow the part of you that knows better to guide and protect you. Return to your perfect self and you will find the true kingdom of God and everything you need. Where? Inside yourself!

Chapter II

Memories

The world is run by information, and we are all run by information too.

My teacher, Dr. Ihaleakalá Hew Len, says that we come with the whole thing. Do you know what he means by this? He means that, when we are born, we come full of memories from our ancestors and the past. So things and situations are never what we think they are. You must remember when you argue about something that is happening right now, it has nothing to do with that current moment because it is really just your memories replaying.

Let me give you an example. When you go to the movies, you know the movie is not on the screen. It is in the back, in the projector. Well, it's the same in life. People and situations are like screens, and we certainly love talking to screens. We are very good at that. We try to convince the screen that we are right. We want the screen to change, but the screen cannot do anything. Screens don't change. If we want things to change on our screen, we need to change. The movie is in us. We are the projector.

Why do memories replay? They show up to give us the opportunity to take 100% responsibility and let go. When we let go, we give Divinity (God) permission to erase those memories and we set ourselves free. In fact, what we call problems are really opportunities. Life is about opportunities to grow and find who we really are, because we have forgotten who we are, why we are here, and what we came to do. We came to this life to remember who we are and make amends. Yes, to correct errors. That is exactly what Ho'oponopono, a very ancient Hawaiian art of problem solving, does. We make amends by taking 100% responsibility and saying, "I am sorry, please forgive me for whatever is in me that has created or attracted this."

Please let me explain here, responsibility is very different from guilt. I am not saying we are guilty. I am saying we are responsible. Yes, we attract everything in our life.

We all go around life trying to figure out what our purpose is. I have news for you. Your purpose is to clean (Ho'oponopono) and let go of anything that is not you. You are not your memories. You are beyond them, but you are responsible for cleaning up your stuff. As Shakespeare would have put it, "This is a big stage, and we are all great actors!"

I imagine right now you are trying to figure this out, but there is nothing here you need to know or understand. Think about it. While you are on your computer working with a program, do you have any idea how many other programs are running in the background? Still, you do not need to know or understand everything that's going on in order to use your computer. All you need to know is that there are programs and they are running. In your reality, you might not understand why or where things are coming from, or why certain things are showing up in your life. And you don't need to know. Your only job is to let go.

For example, when something comes up between you and another person, what happens is not about you or the other person. It is just memories. You don't even need to talk, discuss the issue, or make anybody wrong. Remember, when you see the other person or the problem, you are not truly "seeing" them. You see only the memories of that person or that problem. We always see things through a smoke screen and never see clearly. Everything is tainted by our memories, our judgments, our beliefs, what we think is right, or how we think things should be.

Our only job is to let go. When we do this, whatever gets erased from us gets erased from the other person or the circumstance. People and circumstances will actually change, but it's not really they who change. It is you. As you let go of your memories of people, you will see and experience them differently. So, the next time something comes up in your life, be sure to see it as a blessing, an opportunity to let go, make amends, and to set yourself free. Right now you are a slave. You might think you are free, but you are a slave to your memories and programming, because they tell you what is good and what is bad, what is correct and what is incorrect. The intellect puts labels on everything, but there is no right or wrong. The mind thinks it knows, but it knows nothing. The intellect's only job is to choose; let go or engage, let go or have the last word. To be or not to be, that is the question.

 *Erasing*

Letting go is often mentioned as necessary for spiritual growth, but this can be a scary process. In this book and elsewhere I specifically mention that we must clean and "erase" our memories and programming in order to achieve true joy and inner peace.

Many times during my workshops and classes people ask things such as, "What if I don't want to erase this memory? What if it is a good memory and I don't want to let it go? What is going to happen if I erase? I might be alone. How will I survive?" Many people are afraid of letting go.

Relax!! First of all, let me tell you this: You have A LOT of memories that need to be cleaned and erased. Second, erasing the memories that don't work in your life will open more doors and bring new opportunities. It will bring more people to help and support you and, yes, more people to clean with!

Thank God you are not the one in charge of deciding what memories get erased. Your only job is to give permission. Once you decide to take 100% responsibility for whatever is in you that is creating or attracting certain situations or people into your life, the part of you that knows better, created you, and knows you better than anybody else -some of us call it God- will know what memories you are ready to let go.

One common question is, "Why can't we let go of all the memories at once? You just have to say, Okay, I know. I realize I am 100% responsible. I am willing to say, 'I'm sorry, please forgive me for whatever is in me that has created this.' Now, please remove them all!!"

Well, it's not that simple. It's important to realize that our bodies are memories too, and if God were to remove all our memories at once, our bodies would be unable to withstand it. My teacher, Dr. Ihaleakalá Hew Len, says if this were to happen, our bodies would look like prunes. The part of us that is perfect knows exactly what we are ready to let go and will erase those memories for us. So, isn't it wonderful to know that you don't even need to know what you are letting go?

Yes, it is all about "memories." When something comes up in your life, it is just a memory replaying. In a certain circumstance, you might think you are spiritually processing and clearing something related to a specific person, or the government, or the house, or money, but in reality you never know what you are cleaning with. Only God knows.

Another popular question about the cleaning is, "Do I have to believe in God for this to work?" The answer is NO; you don't have to believe in God. It works anyway, for everybody. Our task is to give permission. You do not need to know or understand what happens afterwards. All you need to do is trust that something WILL happen.

You might also wonder, "Do I have to mean it? Do I have to feel it?" Let me ask you something. When you push the delete key on the keyboard of your computer, do you mean it? When you do it, do you have to "feel" something? Or better yet, do you smile while you do it? Do you feel compassionate? No, you don't have to mean it or feel it, and you don't even need to understand what happens after you press the delete key. Have you ever tried to understand how a program downloads to your computer? It works without understanding the process. Letting go doesn't need to be understood; just hit the key by using tools like "thank you," "I love you" or "I am sorry, please forgive me for whatever is in me that created this." Everything after that is automatic.

In Ho'oponopono we always say, "Please, Just do it. Just say it." Taking 100% responsibility for the memories and programs that are not working in your life and letting go of these memories and programs will have you attracting the right things at the right time. Since the intellect will never understand it, all you need to know in your heart is that, when you allow this to happen, when you give permission, when you ask for help, help ALWAYS comes. You must be willing to trust and know in your heart that every time you give permission, the transmutation (something that only God can do) takes place. Every time! Guaranteed!

****
Your interaction is requested about the chapter you just read...
Visit *http://www.hooponoponoway.com/theeasiestwaytolive/*
and ask any question you have or share your candid feedback.

Also find me on Facebook at: *www.Facebook.com/MabelKatz*

Mabel Katz
****

Chapter IV

The Power of Thank You

Gratitude is immensely important. Just think of all the things you can be grateful for. Can you read? Are you able to hold this book and turn the pages all by yourself? If you are reading this, you can see. You are breathing. You woke up this morning and saw the sunlight, heard the morning sounds, and smelled the air. Each moment we have on earth is full of opportunity. It is a true gift. Thank you, God!

Sometimes we do not realize how lucky we are. Please, stop for a moment and look at the sky, a tree, or the smile on a child's face. Smell the roses.

When you start appreciating the beauty around you, more good things will come your way. The key is to focus on what you have. We all tend to forget the immense power of gratitude and take so much for granted because we are too busy focusing on what we don't have instead of being thankful for what we do have. Please realize this and be grateful that you are free!

In Ho'oponopono, we use "Thank you" as a cleaning tool. The idea is that, every time we say thank you, we are taking 100% responsibility, letting go, and giving the Universe permission to bring us all the good we deserve. When we repeat "Thank you," we erase, clean and let go of the memories that don't serve us anymore. We allow inspiration to enter our lives with the perfect ideas and solutions to our problems. That's right. Did you know that sometimes what you are looking for is just one thank you away? Many times we give up just when something big is about to happen.

It is much easier to feel grateful when we let go of expectations and surrender to the flow of life. Many times we don't feel gratitude because we create expectations for everything, even for the process of spiritual cleaning itself. In this case, since we think we know what is best for us, we believe we know how the cleaning has to work. We think we know when things should happen and how they should happen. Then, we become angry and close our hearts when reality doesn't match our expectations, and as we do this, we become completely unable to see the wonder of life and feel thankful for having the opportunity to be in it. However, being open, flexible, and letting go of expectations is the secret.

You might find yourself in difficult and painful situations, but the truth is God never gives you more than you can handle and is always there to support you no matter what you are going through. What happens is we immediately go into judgment and ask the Universe, "Why me?" instead of saying, "Thank you, God, for trusting me and giving me this opportunity."

Gratitude changes our vibration, our energy. When we synchronize with heartfelt thankfulness, we immediately feel at peace and become magnets for better things. Conversely, when we think negatively, we see only problems and not the solutions.

Saying thank you is also a way of "letting go." It closes doors, and many times we need to close some doors in order to allow others to open. There is opportunity all around you. Some opportunities are very close, just waiting for you to let go, so say thank you as often as you can, mentally and verbally. It works every time. You don't have to feel it or mean when you are doing it to clean.

"Thank you" is pressing the delete key on your computer. It is turning the other cheek, the cheek of love. And, what we can be sure of, is that love can heal it all.

ಬ◆ಬ

****
Your interaction is requested about the chapter you just read...
Visit *http://www.hooponoponoway.com/theeasiestwaytolive/*
and ask any question you have or share your candid feedback.

Also find me on Facebook at: *www.Facebook.com/MabelKatz*

Mabel Katz
****

Chapter V

The Intellect Was Not Created for the Purpose of Knowing

Somehow we have become confused. We believe we are supposed to fill our intellect with knowledge, but the intellect was given to us to choose between thinking and engaging or letting go.

We have become so entrenched in the belief that the intellect's purpose is storing and understanding information, that we base our sense of identity on this idea. Our intellect thus tries to become something that it is not and is always pushing us to be something that we are not meant to be.

In order to break this cycle, we need to realize that we are wise by nature, and that our wisdom does not reside in the intellect. Our creativity is not in our intellect either. Creativity is our natural state. It comes and works in ways that we cannot explain. In reality, our ideas and actions come only from Inspiration or memories.

Now, Inspiration can only come when you are empty and open. It cannot come when you are talking, thinking or worrying. In order to achieve your maximum potential, you must become like a child again, the wise child that you are. You must trust that you are guided and protected when you are not thinking or worrying and be open to all possibilities. You need to go back to your roots, to the time before you became so educated that you lost track of who you really are.

We are the ones complicating our existence. We are the ones thinking we know what is good for us and we make lists of what we want to attract, how much and when, when in fact we don't have a clue of what is good for us, and on top of that, who are we making those lists for? We actually make lists for the Creator, who knows us better than anyone else and knows what we need and when we need it. We are very arrogant, indeed.

Think of nature. Look at the flowers for example. There is no way we humans can create such beauty. We need to admit there is a Divine intelligence. Think of your body. You do not need to think how to breathe or how to make your heart pump. We are surrounded by Divine miracles.

My teacher Ihaleakalá once told me a Hawaiian story of creation that goes like this: When God created the Earth and put Adam and Eve here, he told them that this was paradise and that they didn't have to worry about anything. He said He would provide them with everything they needed. He also told them that He would give them a gift, the opportunity to choose, to make their own decisions, that He would give them the gift of **free choice**. And so, He created the apple tree. He told them, "This is called 'thinking.' You do not need it. I can provide everything for you. You should not worry, but you can choose to follow me or to take your own path (think)."

I would like to make clear that the problem was not the eating of the apple, the problem was not taking responsibility and saying, "I'm sorry." When God asked, Adam said, "She made me do it." And so this is how Adam had to go in search of his first job. Just like Adam, we are always biting the apple. We always think that we know best. We do not realize that there is another way, an easier way.

Anthony De Mello put it simple, "When you become conscious and aware, you become wiser. That is what you call real self-growth. Understand your pride and it will drop - what results will be humility. Understand your unhappiness and it will disappear - what results is the state of happiness. Understand your fears and they will melt - the resultant state is love. Understand your attachments and they will vanish - the consequence is freedom."

Return to the wonder and awe of your childhood. Use the intellect for its intended purpose instead of allowing it to drive you mad. Once you open your heart and cease trying to control reality, wonderful things will begin to pop up all around, and you will recover your sense of joy and freedom.

 *Everything Starts With a Thought*

We create with our thoughts. Everything has to be thought of first in order to exist, to manifest. Somebody had to think of writing this book before it actually appeared and somebody had to think that walking on the Moon was possible before it could actually happen. Everything started from a thought before it showed up in the material world.

Thoughts are extremely powerful, and unfortunately, most of the time they are tainted by our beliefs, emotions, and attachments. We do not think on a blank slate, free from preconceptions, biases, fears, and judgments. Everything we think of is based on our memories, our programming. How does this come about?

When we were kids we heard and saw things. Perhaps people did or said things to us, and based on these experiences, we made certain decisions. At a certain point, we started to believe reality was a certain way and made it that way. We got caught in this cycle of perpetually reproducing what we believed. As you may have guessed already, this leads to a considerable amount of confusion and unhappiness.

We are very attached to our opinions, but we are not aware of the millions of beliefs we hold, and many of these are conflicting. On top of that, we have a lot of other memories from the past that are playing a very important role in the decisions we make and what we attract to our lives.

The only foolproof way to create is through inspiration. But in order to come from inspiration (perfect unbiased ideas), you must be at zero. You must go back to the Void, where you came from. When you are at zero, there is no thinking, no blaming. You are an open channel. The most amazing things happen at zero. Inspiration brings new ideas, new information. Like the guy that invented the Internet, he doesn't know where he got the inspiration from, it just happened. When you are at zero you are open to the flow. You allow Inspiration to guide you and take you. Ideas just come. In this place, you are guided and protected. At zero is when all things are possible and anything can happen, including miracles.

You may wonder, "How do I know this?" Well, many times you will not know if you are coming from memories or inspiration. Your job is simply to keep cleaning (letting go) and thus increasing your chances of drawing your ideas from inspiration. Just keep doing as much cleaning as you can. You will perhaps still engage and get attached to situations. Most of us do. Just keep cleaning, because the ultimate goal is to be as open as possible and receive inspiration moment by moment. Doors will now begin to open as many more opportunities come your way. If you are busy worrying, thinking, coping, and complaining, you will not be in the flow and you will miss these opportunities!

So, here it is one more time. You are making decisions 24 hours a day. Realizing this truth is *The Easiest Way* – like the name of my first book. If you are willing to take 100% responsibility, you can truly set yourself free!

Chapter VII

Become a Child Again

"Truly, I say to you, unless you turn and become like children, you will never enter the kingdom of heaven. Whoever humbles himself like this child is the greatest in the kingdom of heaven." (Matthew 18:3-4)

"Blessed are the pure in heart, for they shall see God." (Matthew 5:8)

When we were kids, we knew better. We were really wise. We lived in the moment and played with abandon and joy. We had little judgment and found wonder in everything we saw. Our hearts were open and pure. We were aware that we had been created unique and that there was something that we could do better than anybody else.

Whatever this gift was, we enjoyed it. We drew, ran, told stories, or sang. We took pleasure in our natural gifts.

Sadly, very early in life we learned to lie. We let go of our natural knowing because it was not okay with others, and we did not want to be different. As children, we were constantly seeking to "belong." Thus, we learned to pretend to be someone that we were not. We stopped forgiving and learned how to put others first.

Society quickly teaches us that love is not unconditional, so we become people pleasers because we think that's what we need to do to survive. Slowly, what others think of us becomes incredibly important, and we start looking for approval outside. We become masters at comparing ourselves to others and seek perfection according to external parameters beyond our control. Once we learn these lessons, we feel miserable most of the time.

Because of this intensive negative training we undergo for years and years, it takes some work to return to our natural childlike state of grace. We can only achieve this when we let go of our memories, especially the ones that tell us that we know it all.

Let me remind you that the intellect has not been created to know, but to choose. Whether you know it or not, you are choosing all the time. No matter how many degrees you have or how much money, or what kind of family you come from, you really don't know anything, and until you realize this, you won't have a chance. To return to a state of grace, you must let go of your arrogance and become more humble. For some of us, this means letting go of a lot of accumulated knowledge and university degrees, because only when we erase our old memories can we again be pure of heart.

It's peculiar how we feel superior for example to a chair, but the only difference is that the chair doesn't have free choice. However, this is the only real difference between the chair you are sitting on and you; the chair knows who it is, and you don't. The chair doesn't question itself. It never wonders,

"Am I a chair or a love seat? Am I made of wood or stainless steel?" The chair knows, but we don't have a clue of who we are.

We have three parts: The conscious mind (intellect or mother aspect), the subconscious mind (our inner child), and the superconscious mind (the father aspect of us). Our relationship with our inner child is the most important one in this lifetime, since the inner child holds all the memories and makes the connection to the superconscious mind when we do the cleaning (Ho'oponopono). The superconscious is the part of us that is perfect and knows exactly who it is. It is connected to the whole Cosmos and Divinity, the Creator.

We have a lot to clean to go back to being kids again, but waking up is the first step on this trip, and the voyage is well worth the effort, because once we know better, we can make better choices. We can choose to let go, reconnect with our wisdom, and go back to trusting our hearts.

Your heart doesn't lie. It will tell you what is right for you, and you shouldn't do anything that doesn't feel right in your heart. Consult your heart before making any decisions and before every move you make. Go back to being a child of God. Return to that state in which you know better. You know you don't need to worry about anything because you are not alone. Trust the wisdom of your heart and go back to being the wise child you already are.

****
Your interaction is requested about the chapter you just read...
Visit *http://www.hooponoponoway.com/theeasiestwaytolive/*
and ask any question you have or share your candid feedback.

Also find me on Facebook at: *www.Facebook.com/MabelKatz*

Mabel Katz
****

Chapter VIII

Forgiveness

There is nothing like forgiveness to heal the soul, open new doors and grow. Although forgiveness may seem difficult, the truth is we were born with that quality, and as we grew, we were programmed and taught not to forgive. Pay attention to children and you'll notice how easily and quickly they let go of a grudge.

Self-forgiveness should be first, as it is a must to accept and love ourselves just the way we are. We must realize whatever we did or didn't do, whatever we said or didn't say, we did it because we didn't know better. We must learn to treat ourselves with kindness and compassion. If we don't forgive, love and accept ourselves, how can we expect others to do it?

If you are upset with yourself, it is not really you upset at you, but your reactions from and to your memories, which control you without you even knowing. The same happens when you are upset at another person. Your discomfort has nothing to do with that person. It is completely dependent on your replayed memories. What you are affected by is not what they did to you, but rather how you reacted to what they did. If you think about it, not everybody reacts to situations and people the same way you do. It all depends on your "perception," which is also controlled by your memories! Everything is about memories replaying. It is important to keep in mind that others do things because they too are manipulated and controlled by their memories.

Your only responsibility and power is to let go of those memories. Nothing much changes when you talk, explain or try to be right. Let me remind you, when you do not forgive, you are not hurting the other person, you are only hurting yourself. So, if you want to be free, forgive and let go. Say "Thank you" (in your heart) to the person that hurt you because he or she just showed up to give you one more chance to let go. Have you ever heard this famous phrase: "What you resist persists"? This is absolutely true. When you let go, the other person will let go too, because it takes two to tango.

When something happens, you are always 100% responsible. Something inside of you has attracted the situation. This may seem foreign or very hard to entertain, but there is something inside of you attracting certain situations or people, and they treat you the way you treat yourself. We haven't been taught to forgive, love and be good to ourselves first. But in reality, when we love ourselves, we attract others who love us too.

I imagine you might feel outraged to read this if you were raped or abused. I would like to ask you to reconsider. Perhaps you are an advanced soul that chose to live this experience. Maybe you were paying an old debt that you weren't aware you had. Whatever it was or is, in order to overcome obstacles and set yourself free, you must be willing to take 100% responsibility and accept there is a blessing in each situation, even if you cannot see it that way yet.

There are many women out there who were "victims" or abused and are now great speakers, motivators, or very successful entrepreneurs. They are out there making a difference. How is this possible? It is possible only because they decided to stop blaming and seeing themselves as victims and instead learned and grew from their experience. God never gives us anything we cannot handle. If you keep seeing yourself as a victim, you don't have a chance.

God is right there to give you the help and support, if you ask. Remember, God gave you free choice. So you must ask. You must give God permission to help you. Yes, you are free to choose. If you are tired, frustrated and feeling hopeless, you can choose to change anytime. I sincerely hope you decide to change, forgive, and set yourself free. Remember, you don't need to talk to anybody or tell the other person you forgive them. Forgiveness is a gift to you. To experience the true miracles of forgiveness, all you need to do is forgive in your heart and let go.

Chapter IX

 *Expectations*

Expectations are also memories. They come from the part of us that thinks it knows better and tells us what the correct results are, how things should be, and what is right and wrong. It's very hard not to have expectations, but when they come up, we let them go and clean, so we can be open, like a child, and thus allow the best possible things to happen. We never know where things are going to come from when we let go of expectations.

In this sense, Ho'oponopono is like magic. Really! When we practice Ho'oponopono without expecting certain results, we can experience that magic. That is why many times, when using Ho'oponopono, we say: "Expect miracles," but we clean and erase this too, so we can really see the miracles. In our minds, we might think we know what the miracle should be and how it should show up. True miracles don't come with expectations; they just show up, magically.

You see, we tend to analyze everything through certain filters. These filters are our attachments, beliefs, and fears. Perception is a key element in our reality, but we don't realize we do not see reality but rather what our filters allow us to perceive. We don't see the big picture, and so we miss opportunities because we blindly believe what our filters show and tell us. We live in a world that we create based on our memories and beliefs. The Universe keeps moving and changing, but we are stuck on the things we have decided to believe. The worst part is that, in accordance with the law of attraction, we find nothing but events and people who assure us that our views are right and we are victims of the circumstances. We are trapped in a viciously insane circle. Like Albert Einstein said, "Insanity is doing the same thing over and over again and expecting different results."

In reality, our only job is to let go and be open to receive. It's like going back to childhood. Do you remember those days? Then we were always willing to play, dream and laugh. Pay attention to children. When something doesn't go their way they get upset, which is extremely hard to avoid, they let go way faster than adults, and soon they are back to playing, dreaming and laughing. Children live in the moment. They don't dwell on the past and don't worry about the future. So that's the key. Let go of those programs that tell you what you should expect and go play like a child again, with little memory or preconceived expectations.

If you are willing to be open and flexible and let go of what you think is right, you will be able to see a Universe and things around you that were always there, but you didn't notice because you expected things to be a certain way. Expectations are born of our attachment to things, people and places. We create our own prisons. We are our own slaves.

Set yourself free. Let go of your attachments and your expectations of achieving certain outcomes. Accept things as they are and as they are presented. The secret is to be free, and that means realizing you do not need anything or anybody. Then, you can enjoy everybody and everything. Know that the Universe is perfect and is as it should be. The only way to do this is to be present and observe life with the curiosity of a child, free of judgments or opinions. When you learn to be in the present and observe without judgment, you will become immensely happy, and this happiness will not depend on things working out the way you expected. You will flow with the river of life, becoming that flow, and you will experience serendipity, a magical synchronicity where incredible things just happen.

The next time something unexpected happens, stop, take a deep breath, and look inside. Look at yourself. When things don't go your way, just observe the situation without engaging with it, knowing that the power it has over you is fueled only by your memories, your beliefs. When you let go of your expectations, you will find the peace you are looking for, the peace that is beyond understanding. Your happiness will no longer depend on having things your way.

Chapter X

Letting Go

What happens when we let go? When we let go, we allow the part of us that knows better to take care of our problems. God gave us free choice, so we can choose to do it our way or His way.

But how do we let go?
We have many different tools to let go, but no matter which one we use, essentially what we are doing is taking 100% responsibility and saying, "I am sorry; please forgive me, for whatever is in me that has created this." When we decide to take 100% responsibility and clean, Mana or Divine Energy immediately comes down and erases memories.

What gets erased? We do not know and we do not need to know. It doesn't matter what memories get erased. The part of us that knows better knows which memories we are ready to let go.

You may wonder who does the erasing. Well, it's not us. We only give permission. Essentially it's very similar to what we do when we download a program to our computer or click on an icon on the desktop. We don't need to know or understand what happens after that. We just need to click. With spiritual cleaning it's the same. We click on the icon (by saying "thank you" for example), and then the part of us that knows better takes care of the rest.

Sometimes we may think we are cleaning with certain situation, certain persons, and that may very well be what pushed our buttons and triggered our cleaning, but we truly don't know what we are cleaning with, and we do not need to know for the process to work.

We are perfect, but our memories are imperfect. Everything in our life is an opportunity to let go, a chance to erase a memory or program that is replaying in our mind, so we can experience our perfectness, no longer controlled by the past, at one with the goodness of the Universe.

Letting go is realizing we are here to find out who we really are and set ourselves free. We are not here to make money, own houses, have cars or find the perfect relationship. All of that may come, and much more easily when we let go, but the true purpose of life is to master detachment, and again, set ourselves free. Enlightenment is the realization that the happiness we seek doesn't depend on what we have or what we want. By setting ourselves free from ourselves and attachments we can be happy and at peace right here, right now.

Then, why is it so hard to let go?
It is difficult because we don't know who we really are. We believe it depends on having certain possessions, certain people in our lives, or certain status to be worthy. We become so accustomed to this belief that we decide to believe it is real. This is what we know, so we do not want to wake up; we would rather suffer than trust the unknown.

Paradoxically, my own experience is that, when you let go of what you want, you receive more than you ever dreamed of. I am not saying it is easy, but it really works. Trust and let go, and be ready for the miracles, because when you let go of what is not working for you, there is a great reward. Wake up and realize you can be happy with just yourself! Your happiness does not depend on anybody or anything.

The world is run by data, and so are we. Much of this data replays in the form of memories in our conscious and unconscious mind, and most of the time, we are not even aware of it. The only way to set yourself free and find the joy and peace you seek is to let go of the data, thus allowing inspiration (perfect data) to come and guide you in the right direction.

Realize your programs (data) are controlling you. You can only set yourself free from their control when you let go. Only then, will you be in the right place at the right time.

****

Your interaction is requested about the chapter you just read...
Visit *http://www.hooponoponoway.com/theeasiestwaytolive/*
and ask any question you have or share your candid feedback.

Also find me on Facebook at: *www.Facebook.com/MabelKatz*

Mabel Katz

****

 *Judgments*

Have you ever noticed that sometimes you go somewhere and see a person sitting there that you don't even know but you have a strong reaction and tell yourself, "I am not sitting next to that person"? In all likelihood, this feeling is fueled by a memory replaying in your programming. It's the result of a judgment based solely on a memory you have. You do not have a clue of what is really going on.

My teacher Ihaleakalá once told me that, as he was watching a couple kissing and hugging each other, he could also see their inner children fighting each other. We can be communicating at the same time in different ways with people, without even knowing it. That is why we don't actually need to communicate to people verbally to change a relationship, because when we clear our personal memories and let go, whatever gets erased from us gets erased from everybody else.

Unfortunately, we see life, events, and people through our memories and "think" we know. We spend an inordinate amount of time suffering because of the way we interpret reality. We often prefer to feel self-righteous than to be happy and at peace. However, if we want to set ourselves free, we need to start letting go of our reality distorting preconceived ideas so we can see things as they are, as God sees them. Things are not good or bad, correct or incorrect. They just are. We put the labels on reality.

Even when we receive a compliment such as, "You are so good at this," or "You are beautiful," it is up to us to receive or reject it. Many times we don't even believe in it. We put ourselves down by saying, "Anybody can do that." We may even have a voice in our head saying things such as, "If he only knew the other part of myself, he wouldn't think I'm so great." Other times, we become attached to a person who compliments us because the compliments make us feel better about ourselves and then we "need" the person in order to feel alright with ourselves. The world can crumble if that same person then says something negative about us. We place an unreasonable amount of significance on our own and other people's judgments.

In reality, our and other people's judgments are just like information on a monitor. The information shows up just to give us another chance to let something go. It's merely data to erase. These events give us the opportunity to say, "I am sorry for whatever is in me that has attracted this into my life." Our job is simple. All we have do is press the delete key! We have to stop talking to the data on the monitor. Let's not waste our precious time. There is nothing the monitor can do, so just let go.

Just be aware that these programs are playing all the time, even when it looks like nothing is happening, that is why you have to be letting go all the time.

So, when stuff comes up, look at yourself! There is nobody else out there. Just set yourself free from all judgment. Observe, and don't get attached to a particular interpretation of events so you can see them as they really are. If you are looking for happiness and peace, let go of your opinions and judgments.

Please wake up, look, observe and realize you are addicted to thinking, judging, having opinions, believing that you know it all. This may not sound easy, but it can be done. Through Ho'oponopono, God gives us the possibility of letting go at a level that would have otherwise taken us thousands of lifetimes to achieve. Ho'oponopono cleaning is like paying off debt, like putting money in the bank that pays very good interest.

Be willing to let go. You can do it! It doesn't pay to judge. It pays to let go.

※◆※

****

Your interaction is requested about the chapter you just read...
Visit *http://www.hooponoponoway.com/theeasiestwaytolive/*
and ask any question you have or share your candid feedback.

Also find me on Facebook at: *www.Facebook.com/MabelKatz*

Mabel Katz

Chapter XII

****

Riding One Horse

My first metaphysical book was written by a very famous Venezuelan author who used to say something like this, "Many will come. You will recognize them by their fruits." She also said, "No matter who is teaching or talking, you have to look beyond the person."

This brings me to my point. It is very important to keep one thing in mind. What matters is the message, not the messenger. But no matter what, you must always follow your heart, and more importantly, no matter who is presenting the information to you, ALWAYS take what feels right in your heart and discard what doesn't.

It is very important to ride only one horse if you want to see results faster. Your subconscious mind or inner child (your Unihipili, as we call it in Ho'oponopono) can do the cleaning for you the same way he/she does your breathing, but he/she will not do it if you are jumping from one teaching to another, or if you practice many different modalities. Why? Because your inner child gets totally confused, and when a problem shows up, he/she doesn't know what to do, which technique or training you would like to use this time. Jumping from one horse to the next can cause you to miss great cleaning opportunities.

It is not easy for anyone to clean all the time because we are addicted to thinking and reacting. We are asleep, on automatic pilot. Our memories and programs are working and making choices for us all the time. We have to actually be conscious in order to choose to let go (clean) instead of reacting. Our inner child will only do this cleaning automatically, if he/she sees that we are committed and we ride only one horse, meaning in this case that we only practice "cleaning."

Just remember that your inner child observes you. He/she doesn't listen to you, but rather looks at your actions. That is why, no matter how much positive thinking, affirmations and visualizations you do, your inner child (the part that manifests reality in your life) will not be able to attract what is right and perfect for you because you are blocking the way. Don't forget that, while you are thinking positive (manipulating the 15 bits of information per second that you can consciously perceive), the other 11,000,000 bits of unconscious information per second are running in the background, saying things such as: "I am not good enough; I have to work hard for my money; Money is dirty," etc., etc. We are not consciously aware of these thoughts, but our inner child (our subconscious mind) is the one storing the 11,000,000 bits and he/she knows where they are downloaded!! This is one of the reasons why your inner child is your best partner.

Affirmations and visualizations are kindergarten stuff. If you just woke up and are realizing the power of your thoughts, please keep playing, but if you are tired of going around in circles, please know you can stop the cycle. Your job is TO BE yourself and let go.

In Ho'oponopono we come from love. We love our enemies (our memories replaying inside of us). We do not resist them. We do not force our inner child to think or feel in a certain way, or to manifest certain things. I have called Ho'oponopono the easiest way because, if you practice, you will experience freedom, happiness, and peace beyond understanding, and the only thing you need to do is to let go of your expectations and attachments to certain outcomes.

Don't get me wrong. It is okay to keep searching, it is okay to keep taking trainings, but once you find what you are looking for, something that works for you, please stick to it and ride one horse!

ॐ ◆ ୡ

****

Your interaction is requested about the chapter you just read...
Visit *http://www.hooponoponoway.com/theeasiestwaytolive/*
and ask any question you have or share your candid feedback.

Also find me on Facebook at: *www.Facebook.com/MabelKatz*

Mabel Katz
****

 *The Chosen Ones*

Most of us tend to feel like victims when unpleasant things happen in our lives. Others see themselves as victims all the time. These people believe the whole world is against them.

The truth is that God loves you always, no matter what.

When you start letting go and trusting, you will discover that you are a chosen one. You are unique. What happens is you start seeing God's work when you let go. You will be amazed because you will start receiving so much more than you ever imagined, and it will come from places you never dreamt of. You will be astonished by how much God loves you and wants you to be happy.

Unfortunately, we are our own worst obstacle in life and we tend to blame it on others. Many times we blame God for our unhappiness or lack of, but God is only waiting for us to give Him permission to solve our problems. Once we do this, we allow God to give us what is right and perfect at each moment. Let me remind you that you do not know what is right and perfect for you! But if you trust and let go, you will be amazed by what God has in store for you.

One thing you can be certain, if you give God permission, you will always have what you need when you need it, not a minute before or after. I know sometimes this can be scary, but here is where the trusting part really plays a very important role. When you trust, you will begin to feel special.

I'd like to tell you a story.
When I separated from my husband after twenty years of marriage, I left only with what I had on. A friend suggested that we move in together because

by combining our incomes, she and I together would qualify for a nicer and bigger place. This was in California. Two days before signing the lease, my friend called to tell me she had changed her mind and was going to move to Arizona. As I started my cleaning (letting go), immediately a thought came to me, call the real estate agent and ask her if the lease could be put in just my name, so I would be the sole responsible party. To my amazement, she agreed, and not long after moving into the house, I started getting work from everywhere. Soon, I realized I was able to pay the rent on my own and didn't need to share my house with another person.

Eight months after that, the owner of the house called to say he wished to sell the property. He explained that since he knew I liked the house, he wanted to give me priority, but if I was not interested, I would have to move out by September.

Of course I wanted to buy the property and stay there, but how? I didn't have money for the down payment, and since I'm an accountant, I knew very well I did not fulfill the requirements to get a loan. My intellect was telling me to start packing, but something inside told me that this was not my best option. At that moment I said to myself, "If God thinks this is the place for me, He will find me the loan, because I don't know how to get one." I knew I needed to get out of the way and give permission. The best thing was to let go, trust, and hand the matter over to the Universe.

Two people who had said they might be able to help me get a loan gave up in the process. The lease expired, and I did not get the loan, so I had to call the owner. I decided instead of worrying about what I would say to convince him, I would surrender to the situation with confidence and faith. And so I began to clean (let go), then called him and explained everything. Surprisingly, he said, "That's okay, Mabel. In truth this is not the right time to put the property up for sale. I will extend the lease. Write an extension, fax it to me, and I will sign it." When I finally bought the property, I didn't need to call anybody to get a loan. A new broker called me to offer his help, and before the extension expired he got me the loan!

We feel like the chosen ones when things go our way. One thing we need to realize is, in order to be chosen, we need to first choose to give permission and then detach. We must accept we do not know what is right for us and get out of our own way.

Aren't you tired of seeing yourself as a victim? Haven't you had enough suffering already? The joy and peace you are looking for are not where you think they are. Are you waiting for your neighbor to change? Are you praying for your kids to stop doing drugs and behave? Are you hoping your boss will give you that raise or your husband will be faithful?

You will need to detach from it all to find the peace, freedom and happiness you are looking for. Set yourself free. We are all God's children. We are all the chosen ones. Even though we all look different, we all come from the same Father. The sooner we discover this and decide to let go of our opinions, beliefs and judgments, the sooner we can stop behaving like victims and feel like the chosen ones.

****
Your interaction is requested about the chapter you just read...
Visit *http://www.hooponoponoway.com/theeasiestwaytolive/*
and ask any question you have or share your candid feedback.

Also find me on Facebook at: *www.Facebook.com/MabelKatz*

Mabel Katz
****

 *Emotions*

Emotions are useful survival tools. Fear, for example, signals us to move away or avoid a dangerous situation. But they are also powerful obstacles to our self-discovery and freedom if we cannot let go of them. There is nothing wrong with emotions per se. They are just memories replaying, and as such, they are not real. You must understand this clearly if you want to be free.

Many times an emotion is born from either trying to get something that you don't have, holding on to something that you had and no longer have, or avoiding something you do not want.

Think about it. It's all about attachment! You cannot be happy when you are attached to something or someone to the point you believe your happiness depends on that something or someone. I am not suggesting that you stop loving your kids, your family, or your friends. Love with no attachments. Love without expecting anything in return. You can be caring, reliable and loving parents, partners, and friends without believing that your happiness depends on someone or something external to you. True joy comes from within.

It is important to realize that attachment to our emotions as well as external people, things or circumstances is something we learn in our earliest childhood. It is among the memories that replay in our minds, a very powerful programming. These emotions and attachments may have a strong hold on our soul, but they are not real. They are not who we truly are. Their hold on us is only as strong as our belief in their reality. Once we awaken and understand this, we realize we are the ones who decide what we need in order to feel happy. Therefore, right now you can choose whether you want to be happy and free, or attached and miserable. Remember, even pleasant emotions can be disturbing in the end, as everything has its season, so they too will end, and if you are attached, you will regret their parting.

Can you see how terrible this is? We have created a vicious circle of emotional attachment. We think we need something for our emotional wellbeing, but when and if we get it, we are still emotionally attached to our fear of losing it.

The truth is that nobody and nothing out there can give you emotional wellbeing. It is just you and your programs, your decisions, the things you have decided to believe you need in order to be happy.

Please, stop resisting the truth. Set yourself free. There is nobody out there but your true self. Remember, a problem is not a problem unless you say it is a problem. And the problem is not the problem. How you emotionally react to the problem is the real problem.

I would like to share something with you from the scientific based side of our emotions, with an excerpt from, *My Stroke of Insight,* by Dr. Jill Bolte Taylor. Jill Bolte Taylor, Ph. D. is a Harvard-trained and published neuroanatomist who experienced a severe hemorrhage in the left hemisphere of her brain in 1996. The book documents her rehabilitation as never told from the inside of recovery. The author writes:

I define responsibility (response-ability) as the ability to choose how we respond to stimulation coming in through our sensory systems at any moment in time. Although there are certain limbic system (emotional) programs that can be triggered automatically, it takes less than ninety seconds for one of these programs to be triggered, surge throughout the body, and then be completely flushed out of our bloodstream. My anger response, for example, is a programmed response that can be set off automatically. Once triggered, the chemical released by my brain surges through my body and I have a physiological experience. Within ninety seconds from the initial trigger, the chemical component of my anger has completely dissipated from my blood and my automatic response is over. If, however, I remain angry after those ninety seconds have passed, then it is because I have chosen to let that circuit continue to run. Moment by moment, I make the choice to either hook into my neurocircuitry or move back into the present moment, allowing that reaction to melt away as fleeting physiology.

On an intellectual level, I realized that I could monitor and shift my cognitive thoughts, but it never dawned on me that I had some say in how I perceived my emotions. No one told me that it only took ninety seconds for my biochemistry to capture, and then release me. What an enormous difference this awareness has made in how I live my life.

Another reason many of us may not choose happiness is because when we feel intense negative emotions like anger, jealousy, or frustration, we are actively running on complex circuitry in our brain that feels so familiar that we feel strong and powerful. I have known people who consciously choose to exercise their anger circuitry on a regular basis simply because it helps them remember what it's like to be themselves.

Let me ask you this, how do we achieve genuine joy and peacefulness? If the answer is, you must distance yourself from attachments, emotions, expectations and external things, this is absolutely correct. The simplest way to do this is to take 100% responsibility for your reality by understanding that you are the one choosing your reactions to your emotions.

So, now you know. Just say thank you to your emotions. Let them go and set yourself free.

****
Your interaction is requested about the chapter you just read...
Visit *http://www.hooponoponoway.com/theeasiestwaytolive/*
and ask any question you have or share your candid feedback.

Also find me on Facebook at: *www.Facebook.com/MabelKatz*

Mabel Katz
****

Chapter XV

Living in the Present

Think about it. At this moment you have everything you need. If you are not happy right now it is because you are focusing on the things that you do not have, rather than what you have. It is very hard to live in the present because our memories are continuously taking us to the past or the future. We are hardly ever in the here and now.

Fortunately, we have been granted a number of tools to make the process easier. Among them, three are basic.

The first one is our breath, probably one of the most accessible and effective tools we have. As my dear friend Cyrus Ontiki, a laughing yoga teacher, says, "If you are breathing, you are present. If you are present, you are pleasant." The mere act of conscious breathing instantly brings you back to the present moment. Have you ever noticed that when you go into fear, worry, or anxiety the first thing you do is hold your breath? Practice breathing consciously to increase your ability to stay present, and to improve your health and emotional wellbeing.

Laughter is another wonderful tool. Laugh about your problems. Realize that your problems are just your memories. You can laugh about all the problems you attracted and then let them go. When you are laughing you are also breathing. You are present.

Last but not least is gratefulness. Being grateful for the things you have will bring you to the present and change your vibration and energy right away. Gratefulness allows things to happen fast, in the ways you least expect. When you change your vibration, you change what you attract.

In our minds, we often postpone happiness for the future, believing that there is something missing that would make us happy. We truly think that external circumstances, objects or persons can give us true joy. Wrong! Because you are too busy "thinking," you may not notice the natural underlying joy that is your birthright. You can be happy now!

The past is gone. There is nothing we can do about it, so let go and allow God to bring you what is perfect for you at each moment. The past doesn't repeat itself when we learn to let go.

The future is a mystery and will take care of itself. It depends on the decisions we make in the present moment. Everything can change tomorrow because today we decide to let go instead of reacting, or simply because we are willing to clean and let go of our expectations and/or judgments and opinions and keep our mouth shut! When we do this cleaning, we never know what may be coming down the line. Something unpleasant can be ready to manifest, but does not because we decide to laugh instead of getting upset. When you are willing to take 100% responsibility and know that everything and everybody comes into your life to give you an opportunity to make amends and set yourself free, you make better choices that will definitely affect your tomorrow. Not even God knows the future. You have been given free choice, and God is waiting for you to choose.

Remember, nothing is what it seems. Your reality is completely dependent on your old memories and ingrained programs. So the next time something comes up with anybody, laugh and say, "How interesting, another opportunity!"

We often feel like we carry a load, but if we concentrate on enjoying the present and everything it brings, the load will become lighter and we will laugh more. God has a very good sense of humor and knows us better than anybody else.

Become an observer of reality, instead of a judge. Detachment is your savior. Believe me. Life can be fun and easier than you think. Flow with life, like little children, who have no beliefs or judgments. Be present. Observe what comes up and thank it when it does. If you allow it, life will take care of you moment by moment. Today, tomorrow and always.

****
Your interaction is requested about the chapter you just read...
Visit *http://www.hooponoponoway.com/theeasiestwaytolive/*
and ask any question you have or share your candid feedback.

Also find me on Facebook at: *www.Facebook.com/MabelKatz*

Mabel Katz
****

 *Habits*

Habits are among our worst enemies. We learn how to do something a certain way, and although it may not be working for us, we just keep on doing it, because it has become an unconscious habitual behavior we stored in our memory. We even choose to suffer because it has become a habitual behavior.

Did you know that suffering is optional, that you are actually choosing to suffer? All sorts of things might happen and come your way because that is what life is all about, and you might feel some pain, but suffering is optional.

The problem is not the hurt or the pain, but your reaction to that hurt or pain. Suffering comes from your attachment to a certain outcome. Trying to understand it all with your mind, obsessing, and judging are all habits that cause great suffering. You may believe that these unconscious habitual actions are unavoidable, but the good news is they are not, you can let go of them.

To break habits you need to wake up and start observing what you are actually doing to yourself. You must become conscious and realize you are 100% responsible for whatever happens in your life. You are the decision maker. You choose all the time. You make choices based on your perception and how you see things, and your perception is tainted by your beliefs, opinions and judgments. In other words, you are creating what is happening and you are the only one that can change it.

Start asking the right questions and start exploring in the right places. As you decide to take that first step, things and better opportunities will start coming your way. They say that, when the student is ready, the teacher appears. The Universe is just waiting for you to wake up. Everything starts and ends with you, so you are the only one that can change your habits. Nobody can do it for you. Many times we seek gurus outside of ourselves to tell us how to change, but everything you need to change is inside of you and you only know what works for you.

You might find teachers on your path that will mark a direction to follow and give you some information, techniques, etc., but if you are not willing to try, practice and go for it, nobody can do it for you. Only you can break your patterns and change your destiny. In some instances, you might need to feel great pain in order to get to the point where you say, "Enough is enough."

You must be aware that habits create your destiny. If you don't like the way your life is going, change your habits to change your course. It is easier than you think. Break your habits by opening your mind and your heart to a new possibility, a reality in which you take 100% responsibility for what manifests in your life. Let go of preconceptions, judgments and opinions.

Be willing to leave your comfort zone. Feel the fear and do it anyway. Nobody can do it for you and tell you about it. You must experience it for yourself, and to get there, you might have to do things that are scary, but the results are guaranteed. Doors will open for you every time you leave your comfort zone. Again, feel the fear and do it anyway. I promise you, once you start experiencing the magic of having an open mind, of letting go and letting God, you will see how much easier life can be. You will ask yourself why you didn't do it before.

Understand that maybe you do not know as much as you thought you did. You will have to let go of the old to allow new information to come in. There will be confusion, but that is a good sign. It means something is happening!

Think of your childhood dreams. Realize that you are the one who has decided to believe those are only dreams. Perhaps somebody told you that you couldn't make a living or that you would starve if you pursued those dreams. Challenge those decisions that have become your unconscious habitual beliefs. All of this will be easier when you understand that habits are just your memories and you can let them go. Are you willing to do what it takes to end habits that are keeping you from being happy and feeling fulfilled? Rejection and people telling you that your dreams aren't possible and you should let them go should be your biggest motivation. Be grateful. Do not complain. Do what you love. Work harder. Let go of the bad habits and get out of your comfort zone. Stretch and dare to go for your dreams.

****
Your interaction is requested about the chapter you just read...
Visit *http://www.hooponoponoway.com/theeasiestwaytolive/*
and ask any question you have or share your candid feedback.

Also find me on Facebook at: *www.Facebook.com/MabelKatz*

Mabel Katz
****

 *Addictions*

Addictions are memories, so no matter what our memories are about, we can erase addictions and let them go.

You may be thinking, "But I don't have an addictive personality," or, "I don't have any addictions!" I would like to invite you to reconsider these assumptions.

Did you know that thinking is an addiction? We are addicted to thinking. We truly fear that we cannot function properly unless we "think things out," when in reality, things can flow and work much better if we simply let go and trust the Universe.

Food is another acceptable addiction. It is something we have decided we need or can't live without! Many times we use food to medicate ourselves, like a pain killer. By eating, we often attempt to avoid feeling certain feelings or facing things in our lives.

And, let's not forget shopping! How many times have you gone shopping because buying something nice would make you feel better? Think about it, do you have any of these addictions?

Addictions might take a little bit longer to let go of than other things. If you see the thought form — yes, thoughts are things and have forms — you will realize addictions have hooks. This makes them a bit harder to erase, but it can be done. It is important to be patient and at peace no matter what.

Please don't think your addictions are "bad." Remember, what you resist persists. Try to love and accept your addiction. Show it the other cheek, the cheek of love. Say, "I love you" to the cigarette, to alcohol, to relationships, to your intellect that thinks it knows… Love can heal anything. The only way to let difficult things go is to love them.

Be patient. If you do your part, God will do His, but only at His own pace, at the perfect time, not necessarily at the time you think it should be done. All throughout the process, it is important to steer away from expectations.

It really helps to work with our Unihipili (inner child) on this, because this is our emotional part. He/She is the one that suffers. Fortunately, you can comfort this part of yourself. Talk to your inner child. Tell him/her that it is going to be okay, that you are there with him/her, and remind your inner child that together, you can do it. Assure this part of you that you are not going to abandon it this time and that you are sorry for the times you neglected it.

Remember that you are unlearning, doing a lot of reprogramming, and in order to be successful, you have to be good to yourself. Love and acceptance of yourself is a crucial element of the process. Only with love can we heal.

Once you master this process, you will be able to observe reality from a completely different point of view. You will be more detached, so you will appreciate your addiction as you start appreciating life and the universe of animate and inanimate things around you. And as you realize the addiction is just your memories and you take 100% responsibility, you will finally be able to change it. You will discover that you are not the addiction, but since you did create and attract the addiction, you can also let it go.

The goal is to be happy and at peace with or without the addiction. We must reach a point where we are joyous for no specific reason. Once you know this feeling, you will be able to wake yourself up every time you fall back into the addiction. You will look inside yourself for that peace and happiness you are longing for and realize you do not need the addiction or anything outside yourself to be happy. Once you take 100% responsibility and realize it is not you but your programs that attracted the addition, you will be able to actually say "thank you" to that addiction. You will be grateful for the growth opportunity it provides and will find true joy in your heart because now you know you don't need it anymore and you can let it go.

Remember, you create your reality, so you can change it! Addiction is just another opportunity to grow and find your true self.

****
Your interaction is requested about the chapter you just read...
Visit *http://www.hooponoponoway.com/theeasiestwaytolive/*
and ask any question you have or share your candid feedback.

Also find me on Facebook at: *www.Facebook.com/MabelKatz*

Mabel Katz
****

 *Fear*

Stop the world! I want to get off! Don't you sometimes feel like screaming that? Well, we are now in the middle of the song, so we need to dance until it comes to an end. In the meantime, wake up and see things as they really are. I know it is terrifying to let go of everything we know as real. Fear is inevitable when we let go of the known and embrace the unknown.

The beautiful thing about this process is that everything you are looking for, and what your soul is longing for, resides in this unknown. Sure, you will feel fear when it comes to letting go of reality as you know it, but you must do it anyway. Know that, if you are willing to ask for help, the help will be right there for you. All you need to do is ask, because you have free choice. The Universe cannot intervene if you do not request it. When you practice Ho'oponopono (saying "Thank you" or "I love you" to the fear), essentially what you are doing is asking for help. You take 100% responsibility for your reality and give God permission to take you by the hand, guide you and protect you. Nobody can do it for you. You are not alone. Ask and you shall receive.

Be willing to observe the fear, knowing that you are not that fear. You are above it. By doing this the fear will immediately melt and disappear. As soon as fear goes, in will come inspiration and guide you back to paradise, even if just for one split second! And when the next memory of doubt or fear appears, just keep letting go, moment by moment. When fear shows up, please do me a favor, breathe and laugh. The first thing we do when fear comes up is to stop breathing, so just this small step will go a long way in helping fear go away.

Think about it, you have the possibility of seeing the Universe as God sees it, without fear. It is like seeing for the first time, like a newborn. It is another chance to start over. The happiness you are seeking is behind every "Thank you" and "I love you" you say to fear, doubt, opinions and judgments before you let them go. Be grateful for fear, as it shows up to give you another chance to let go. It is a good alarm clock, telling you it is time to wake up, to do something differently, or maybe it is time to move, to take action. Fear is something we create in our minds, and our belief in it gives it power. As soon as we become aware of this truth, fear simply melts away.

****
Your interaction is requested about the chapter you just read...
Visit *http://www.hooponoponoway.com/theeasiestwaytolive/*
and ask any question you have or share your candid feedback.

Also find me on Facebook at: *www.Facebook.com/MabelKatz*

Mabel Katz
****

Chapter XIX

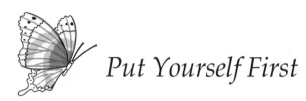

Put Yourself First

As we grow up we are taught that it is selfish to put ourselves first and do what works for us. Thus, we become people pleasers and learn that what others think of us is more important than what we think of ourselves. This is a sad mistake that leads to much unhappiness in our world.

My teacher Ihaleakalá came back from walking one day and told me, *"I am very touched right now because I've just realized that all God is asking us, is to take good care of ourselves and to say 'I am sorry.' That's it!"* It's that simple. All we need to do is stop trying to please others and put ourselves first.

This can be such a scary idea in a society that teaches us to place everything on the outside world, including responsibility for our actions.

Unfortunately, we do things to please others, without realizing that, if it doesn't work for us, it will not work for others. On the other hand, when we put ourselves first, we allow others to put themselves first too. We are allowing them to be themselves. We cannot truly help others if we don't help ourselves first. I'm sure those of you who have traveled on an airline have heard the safety announcement about putting the air mask on yourself first, before helping others. Think about it. What good are we to others if we neglect ourselves to the point we are unable to help them?

Our dependence on the outside world causes us to seek approval in the wrong places. We want others to approve of our decisions and we long for others to love us, but we don't approve of or love ourselves. We often put others first because we are looking for their love and acceptance. Then, once we get their acceptance at the expense of our true identity, we find that we are not happy. Nothing can fill the void left by the denial of not accepting our true selves.

We expect something in return for our favors to others, and then, we get very upset when others don't respond in accordance with our expectations. In this way, we are putting chains on ourselves and others.

In reality, nobody can do to us what we do not allow them to do, nor can anybody do anything that we are not already doing to ourselves. People treat us the way we treat ourselves. It is hard for us to realize this, but we are responsible for whatever we are attracting to our lives. We may not do it consciously, but we do it. Our reality has nothing to do with what others are doing to us; our reality is only what we are allowing. Everything is a reflection of the old memories and programs. We can choose to allow, or we can choose to let go.

So, the only way out of this vicious circle is to put ourselves first in every sense, not only when it comes to taking care of our needs, but also when it comes to accepting the liability. We are the masters of our destiny, and only we can set ourselves free by deciding to accept 100% responsibility, forgive ourselves, let go and give God permission to erase the memories that no longer serve us.

Many times we feel alone and look for company or love in the wrong places. Please know that you are never alone. God is always with you. As my teacher Ihaleakalá says, *"There is nothing like hanging out with God."*

Nothing, absolutely nothing on the outside can make you happy. Everything you find outside of yourself can only give you a temporary satisfaction or thrill. Sooner or later it will go away or you might lose interest, and then you will suffer the loss. So, look inside, where the real kingdom of everything you need is. Learn to truly accept and love yourself, and you will become much more accepting and loving to others.

When you put yourself first, you will go beyond the need for approval and become filled with a joy that is independent of external circumstances.

Chapter XX

Peace Begins With You

We are always waiting for things to work themselves out. We hope things will change, and struggle when we realize we can't mold the outside world according to our whims. Truly, we can't change much on the outside, but we can change the world by changing ourselves. When we are at peace, everything and everybody around us are at peace too.

The way we perceive everything and everybody depends on our memories. As we experience turmoil, fear and anxiety, we can clean with those memories. We can let them go. Now we know better, we know they are just memories playing. As you let go and God erases memories from you, they get erased from everybody else. So, once again, you will find peace of mind when you take 100% responsibility and know that, as you let go of whatever is not you, you will find the peace created by being yourself.

As you start cleaning and letting go of everything that is not you, you will be able to appreciate life in a different way. You will find yourself becoming more observant and present. Suddenly you will notice the trees, the falling leaves, and the ocean in ways you have never seen them before. You will realize you have been blind all this time. Your heart will fill with peace when you become able to observe instead of engaging and reacting to the outside world. When you let go of memories, you will see life as God sees it.

In order to be at peace, it is important to remember that it is not in people's nature to kill, be bad, or do harm. People act this way because they are constantly reacting from memories, and since they are not aware, they cannot avoid it.

When somebody does something that you don't like, you have to be conscious, observe, and know the person is not being himself or herself at that moment. He or she is being moved by memories replaying. So, if you can take 100% responsibility, understanding that it's your memories and be willing to clean, whatever is cleaned from you, will be cleaned from them too.

Remember most of our problems come from our ancestors, and most of what is happening right now doesn't have to do with the present. Everything is just memories.

What do you think would happen in the world if people stopped seeing themselves as victims, blaming, thinking they know what's best, or believing they are always right? The human race is ignorant and asleep. We do not know who we are. What would happen if everyone were willing to take 100% responsibility? Do you think this could create world peace?

Let me tell you a story that actually happened to me. A couple of years ago, I went to teach

Ho'oponopono in Chile. The training was all day Saturday and half day Sunday. During the first break we took on Saturday morning, a Palestinian man came to me and said, "I don't agree with anything you just shared with the class and actually I didn't want to come to this class when I saw you had a Jewish last name." He thought I had nothing to teach him. He went on telling me everything he believed, and when he finished, to his surprise, I told him that I agreed with everything he had said, and that I was going to ask him to be open and flexible, because I thought that we were talking about the same thing and maybe calling it different names. He accepted and decided to stay.

The next morning when he came, he shared the most amazing story with the class about a serious problem (police involved) he had the night before and how he had used one of the tools I had given him on Saturday. He couldn't believe the results. He was amazed how things worked out in a miraculous way. Well, at the end of the class, he gave me a huge (not big), huge hug and screamed, "This is Peace in the Middle East!" I hope you get how profound this is. I didn't need to convince him by talking, or arguing, or being right, or having the last word. I just needed to keep my mouth shut and say, "I am sorry. Please forgive me for whatever is in me that has created this," while he was talking to me. I had to be conscious that he was not out there, that he was part of my own thoughts, my own memories. He had shown up in my life to give me a chance to make it right this time.

If you want freedom and peace, look at yourself and realize that you are building on top of memories. You make decisions based on memories. You make judgments based on memories, and see everything through your memories. You are blind and deaf, but you think you know. Many of the memories come from your ancestors. They are not even yours. Somebody has to clean this up, and forgiveness is the only way. When you don't forgive, you hurt yourself, not others. Also, be willing to forgive yourself for not knowing what you were doing.

Ho'oponopono, this ancient art of problem solving, reminds us that the only reason we are here is to make amends and it is a gift to be here.

Once and for all, we must wake up and say, "I am sorry," not because we are guilty, or sinners, but because we are 100% responsible!

Once you awaken, you become more conscious. You become able to observe without attachment. You realize that the peace you are searching for begins with you.

As Mahatma Gandhi once said, *"Be the change you want to see in the world."*

****
Your interaction is requested about the chapter you just read...
Visit *http://www.hooponoponoway.com/theeasiestwaytolive/*
and ask any question you have or share your candid feedback.

Also find me on Facebook at: *www.Facebook.com/MabelKatz*

Mabel Katz
****

Chapter XXI

Changing Your Life

You can change your life without depending on anybody or anything outside yourself. You don't know this because you have forgotten who you are. Your power is inside, not outside, and it doesn't depend on anything external. It is simpler than you think. If you want to change your life, all you need to do is be willing to take 100% responsibility!

No matter what is going on or what it looks like "life" is doing to us, reality is that we are doing it to ourselves.

What we attract and how we perceive what we experience in life is determined by our own replayed memories, our programming "talking to us." These memories are playing all the time. They are like a CD playing in our mind, whether we are aware of it or not. They tell us what is good and what is bad, what is right and what is wrong. Our intellect thinks it knows better, but it knows nothing. It is not even aware it is controlled by these memories.

When we wake up, we know better. We become more conscious and can make better choices. Our best choice is to stop seeing ourselves as victims, as we are not victims and never will be. If you see yourself as a victim of circumstances, please know that in reality, you are the victim of your own thoughts. There is nobody out there. Everything depends on your perception. You perceive that other people are "doing" something to you, but there is nobody out there. What you really see is your thoughts of others or the situation. Again, there is nobody out there.

Changing may be difficult because playing the victim may have its payoffs. You may categorically deny this, but the only reason we give away our power is that playing the victim is giving us some type of benefit. Perhaps we are getting some attention. Maybe we are too scared to sit in the driver's seat of our life. And unfortunately, we are always going to find people that agree with us and confirm our victimhood. On top of that, our subconscious will do whatever it takes to be right. It will go around attracting people and situations so it can say things such as: "See? I told you. Men are not reliable. Women are bad. Or Money is hard to get." Once we believe something, we will always try to prove that our beliefs are right, and then think we are so unfortunate because we seem to attract a whole bunch of bad things.

However, when things happen, we can choose to let go instead of reacting and stop choosing to see ourselves as victims. Letting go is a conscious choice, a better choice. It allows us to find what we are looking for and more. In the beginning it may seem hard to break the habit, but once we learn how to do it, we discover we are in control, and changing our life becomes easy.

Again, if you want to set yourself free, accept 100% responsibility. It is easy to change what you yourself have created and attracted. Answers will start popping up as soon as you entertain the possibility that maybe there is something inside of you attracting things to your life. The perfect solutions will come. You will recover your power. And better yet, because whatever gets erased from you gets erased from others, you will notice people change, but it's not really them changing. As you change, your reality changes. You will need to talk less to get the results you are looking for because you'll relinquish your need to be right and have the last word. You'll know better and understand that "being right" is not important. Your true identity lies beyond the problems and arguments. Set yourself free from this mindset and you will find peace. As you change, you will notice the world will change too.

We may all look different. Some may seemingly have more challenges, others less, but we all have the same opportunities. We all come from the same source and we are all going back to that source. If you decide to wake up and stop seeing yourself as a victim, you might decide to enjoy life, have fun and go home in a first class cabin. If you prefer to hold on to your blaming, you might have to go home swimming, but in the end, the only thing we can't change is we are all going back HOME.

****

Your interaction is requested about the chapter you just read...
Visit *http://www.hooponoponoway.com/theeasiestwaytolive/*
and ask any question you have or share your candid feedback.

Also find me on Facebook at: *www.Facebook.com/MabelKatz*

Mabel Katz
****

Chapter XXII

Appearance

What stories do we tell ourselves to keep
happiness and wellbeing away? We can be our
own worst enemy! Our bad feelings about our
physical appearance can affect our reality. It affects
our confidence, how we feel about who we are,
and how we perceive what others think of us.

Look in the mirror. What do you see? Do you see
someone that is overweight? Do you have bad feelings
and worries when you hear the word "diet"? Do you
focus on the pain of not eating everything you would
like? But what could be more painful than feeling
overweight, helpless, and uncomfortable?

In Ho'oponopono, we say these are memories replaying, and these memories are immensely powerful. We think we are free, but these thoughts and programs constantly control us. They are always playing in the background. We need to WAKE UP and make better choices. Awareness is curative and it is the first and most important step towards our goals. We have a choice!

Yes, it takes effort to stay on a diet. You see people around you thinking about food all the time; getting together to eat; talking about what and where to eat. Food is a social thing. There is food all around us, everywhere we go. Well, guess what? The people and circumstances in your life are actually a gift. They are giving you the opportunity to see what you need to change, to let go, so you can take charge of your life.

So, how does this work? Essentially, you must become aware and "let go" of these memories. This is impossible to do at the mind level because we are only aware of a minute portion of the thoughts that constantly play in our heads. The best way to "let go" is to take 100% responsibility for the reality we create for ourselves. I use Ho'oponopono tools to constantly "clean" both conscious and unconscious memories and thoughts. My best tool is to say, "Thank you, I love you" to these memories and thus release them.

The process can be much easier if we work with our subconscious mind (our inner child), because this part of us holds these memories. Therefore, the inner child, or Unihipili in Hawaiian, is the part of us that manifests our reality. It is crucial to develop a strong loving relationship of trust with our inner child in order to change our reality, because it can make this journey much easier. Remember, this is the part of you that suffers, it is not you. It is the part of you that is hungry or thinks it cannot survive unless it has some vanilla ice cream!

I would like to share with you what happened to me on my last trip to Japan with my teacher, Ihaleakalá. This was very important for me. I was in Okinawa and I asked for room service. I ordered chicken, and it came with rice, so I told them to replace the rice with vegetables. They said okay, but when they brought my order back, they had replaced the rice with French fries!! I love French fries. I would say they are one of my weaknesses. In the past, I could have never said NO to French fries. I used to eat everybody's left over French fries. Well, let me tell you, I put one in my mouth. I actually got the opportunity to taste it, but I took it out of my mouth and ran with the plate to the bathroom, where I threw the fries away. Yes, I threw them away!! I couldn't believe it myself. The only reason I was able to do that is that I got to the point where I said, "Enough is enough." I made a commitment to myself that I would do whatever it takes to take good care of myself. I promised to stop hurting myself. Our love for ourselves gives us the strength to persevere. I couldn't have done it without the help of my inner child. As I was taking the French fry out of my mouth, I kept reassuring my inner child, "We can do it. It's going to be okay. We are going to be fine."

However, beware. Merely changing your weight or appearance will not solve your problems. These features are on the "outside." What you need to change and let go of are the memories and programs, the things you decided to believe about yourself. Otherwise, your happiness will be temporary. You cannot depend on outside circumstances for your wellbeing. Working with your memories that tell you that you are fat, is essential to achieve true happiness.

My teacher Ihaleakalá says that the food is not what makes us fat. It is our thoughts of the food that make us fat.

Once you start "letting go" of these memories replaying, you will begin to see the results and start choosing better. It's like a chain reaction. When you do the right thing and you feel so good and proud of yourself, you move forward with other things left on the back burner. Thus, you keep feeling better and better, and suddenly you become UNSTOPPABLE.

So, how badly do you want it? Are you willing to do what it takes? It does take hard work to get where you want, but you can choose to practice Ho'oponopono (letting go) and actually see the whole picture and enjoy the process! Take responsibility and let go and you will really find peace and happiness, not only with the way you look and feel, but in everything.

****
Your interaction is requested about the chapter you just read...
Visit *http://www.hooponoponoway.com/theeasiestwaytolive/*
and ask any question you have or share your candid feedback.

Also find me on Facebook at: *www.Facebook.com/MabelKatz*

Mabel Katz
****

 *Happiness*

Our reality includes all our programs, memories, beliefs, attachments, emotions, and expectations. These have been gathered through eons of time. We have been blind and deaf for eons of lifetimes. We are completely drugged, looking for love, approval and appreciation in the wrong places and from the wrong people. We search for success, power and material things, believing this is what will "make" us happy. We tend to try to change people because we think that if they change, we'll be happy. We constantly give our power away by thinking that our happiness depends on other people and external circumstances.

People think of happiness as an experience. If I ask you to describe happiness, you will probably start listing the things, circumstances and people you have or want to have in your life that you believe will "make" you happy. This is because like most people, you probably think happiness comes from having what you want in life. However, although we may feel a fleeting sense of satisfaction when we achieve and attract what we want, true happiness is a state of mind that is not related to cause or effect. In other words, when you are genuinely happy, you can't explain why you're happy. You just are!

As you grew up, you were taught that you "needed" certain things in life in order to be happy, but the truth is you are already happy. You just don't know it. Believe it or not, being unhappy is actually "work" because it is a state of mind created by you.

My teacher Ihaleakalá always says that we are already perfect, but our memories are imperfect. Our memories and programming tell us we need certain external things to be happy, so we tend to attach to things, outcomes, relationships, etc. But even when we manage to have these things, we find that we are still unhappy, because now we struggle to protect what we have; we tap into the fear of losing what we are attached to. On top of that, we always manage to want something else, so very often, when we obtain what we really want, we soon forget how much we wanted it and instead put all our attention on another thing we're missing. There is always something in the way of happiness because we keep focusing on our attachments.

When we feel that we are happy due to something that is happening, an event or person in our life, etcetera, this is not real happiness. What we usually call happiness is merely an experience of happiness, a fleeting feeling of momentary satisfaction.

Fortunately, as soon as we remove the unhappiness created by this self-defeating view of reality, the happiness that lies underneath can shine through. We can do this by becoming conscious that we are not these memories, these constant thoughts that tell us we need external objects, circumstances, or people to feel joy. We can actually choose to be happy. It is essential to be aware that we are the ones creating our unhappiness. Whatever is telling us that we need certain things to be happy is only a memory. Let it go!

True happiness may be rarely felt, but it is easy to recognize. Think back to times when you were happy for no reason. Watch children play and you will see true happiness in their joyous surrender to the present moment. Real happiness is not "caused" by something specific. It is a state of being.

Once you understand your unhappiness, it will disappear because awareness is curative. Being conscious of what you are doing to yourself can set you free. Find opportunities to be yourself. Do what you love. Give back to life. Help others. These things will remind you of the true happiness you have inside, the birthright that is hidden underneath your memories, the misleading preconceptions, constant worrying, judgments, fear, and need to control the outcome. The truth is we are all born happy. This is our natural state.

Please don't fool yourself by thinking that when you have a certain amount of money in the bank, or when that person finally loves you, you'll be happy. Don't waste any more time. Life is short and it is happening now. All you have is the present moment. Choose to be happy now!

****
Your interaction is requested about the chapter you just read...
Visit *http://www.hooponoponoway.com/theeasiestwaytolive/*
and ask any question you have or share your candid feedback.

Also find me on Facebook at: *www.Facebook.com/MabelKatz*

Mabel Katz
****

Chapter XXIV

The Best Time to Talk to People

Do you have problems with other people? Are you frustrated in your relationship, concerned about your kids, or unhappy with your boss? If so, I suggest you talk to them when they are asleep. Believe it or not, this is the most effective way to communicate your message to others. It is very simple. When they are sleeping, you can whisper in their ear, "I love you. Thank you for being in my life." That's it!! Please do not start giving them instructions about how they should behave when they wake up. The only thing people need to hear is that you accept them just the way they are.

I know what you're thinking. Some of these people don't live with you! Trust me, it can still work. If they are not with you when they sleep, you can talk to them when you know they are sleeping. I promise you that they will still get your message.

When we talk to the sleeping individual, we communicate directly with the subconscious mind, which never sleeps. That is the part you want to talk to. It is useless to talk to the person's intellect, because it immediately defends itself. Do not waste your time. I'm sure you've attempted countless conversations and you already know that doesn't work.

Your clarity and awareness will grow as you let go of old memories and preconceptions through the process of cleaning, and as you grow spiritually and become more open and loving, you will bring this clarity and awareness to your relationships. Then, you will start seeing people as they really are, not as you would like to see them. And, as you realize that you are looking at everybody through a dirty glass (tinted by your memories), you will become more conscious that people cannot help doing what they do because they don't know better. In fact, we all do the best we can at each given moment. With this realization, you will naturally communicate better with others and learn that not talking at times is best.

You must become conscious and aware that you are the one placing labels on things, making people wrong, and you do this based on your perception. Realize your perception is based on your beliefs, and your beliefs create opinions and judgments. Your opinions and judgment create the need to be right, but being right doesn't make you happy. As you stop communicating from your own perceptions and stop projecting your need to always be right, you will see that talking to others takes on a whole new light.

So you can decide right now to be happy. You can let go of the need to be right or have the last word. You've probably already experienced the feeling of winning a discussion and you know it is temporary. The feeling you are looking for is inside yourself. You will not find it outside. When you change everything changes.

As you practice this method, you will see that people change, but you are the one changing, not them. Your thoughts of the others have changed, so they "have" to change.

Relinquish the need to talk, to be right or having to defend yourself or your point of view. Love people and accept them just the way they are. Start loving and accepting yourself first and you will notice it will be much easier to love and accept others.

It is quite a wonderful process. As we wake up, we allow others to wake up too. The truth will set you free, and as you become free, others will be freed too, but everything starts with you.

Realize everybody in your life is just your thoughts. A blessing in your life!

ജ ◆ ଓ

****
Your interaction is requested about the chapter you just read...
Visit *http://www.hooponoponoway.com/theeasiestwaytolive/*
and ask any question you have or share your candid feedback.

Also find me on Facebook at: *www.Facebook.com/MabelKatz*

Mabel Katz
****

 *Love*

Oh, how we suffer and pine for what we perceive to be love! We believe infatuation and its attachments are love, and we persist in this view, thus creating endless disappointment. However, true love cannot cause pain. On the contrary, true love is fully accepting and unconditional. It does not depend on external events or circumstances. It is detached from the outcome. Love is just because it is. When we love as God loves, our hearts sing. There are no attachments or expectations. True love sets us free.

We are the ones that decide that, because we have a good time with somebody (pleasure), we are in love, but actually, what we perceive as love is truly infatuation. We deposit our heart on that person, and when we are not with them, we feel incomplete. We literally walk around without a heart!! We become unable to be present and cannot enjoy the moment because we do nothing but concentrate on the object of our infatuation. We become anxious and perpetually unhappy. The same way we confuse money with wealth, we confuse pleasure with love. In our desire to hold on to what gives us a moment of pleasure, we become attached and imprisoned in a vicious circle of constant anxiety.

We definitely need to deprogram ourselves before getting into a relationship. First we need to realize that the love we are seeking cannot come from the outside. Nobody out there can make us happy. Second, nobody is going to love us more than we love ourselves. It is so important for us to love and accept ourselves for who we are. What matters the most is not how others feel about us, but how we feel about ourselves.

In relationships, detachment is a big must. Dr. Michael Beckwith once said, "If you want something, let it go." This is essential. Our attachment is born from our memories, programs, and beliefs. If we say we need a certain person in our life to be happy, that is what we'll believe, and in this belief we become attached. This type of interaction comes from feeling that we "need" outside people to somehow complete us, when the truth is we really don't "need" anything or anybody outside ourselves. We are already complete. Have you ever noticed that you enjoy people more when you don't have any attachment to them?

This might sound complicated, but letting go of attachments can be easier than you think. All you need to do is wake up and realize it's your programs controlling you, making you believe that outside circumstances, people or things will make you happy. There are so many rewards when you learn to detach. You feel lighter and happier, and immediately you start to attract more love than you ever imagined.

Think about it, every instance of unhappiness, jealousy or anxiety is the result of attachment. Detachment sets us free. And by detachment I don't mean inconsiderateness or lack of responsibility. Detachment isn't hurting someone's feelings. This misunderstanding comes from the same fallacy that fuels our definition of love. We believe we should be consistent, responsible and reliable, because "otherwise people won't love us," or we believe this is just the way things are meant to be. In reality, when we take 100% responsibility and truly love ourselves, kindness, consideration and responsibility towards others comes easily, because when we love ourselves loving others comes naturally.

Unfortunately we tend to put everything on the outside world. How many times a day/week/month do you look for approval and acceptance from others? Have you noticed even when you do get their approval, your good feelings and excitement are only temporary? This type of gratification actually produces a sense of emptiness when it wears off. If we don't accept, approve and love ourselves, nobody will do it for us, and until we do, we will never find happiness.

Sometimes we go from one relationship to the next, repeating situations and attracting the same things over and over. This is caused by memories, and they will continue to replay, until we understand that they are just thoughts of ourselves, others and situations programmed in our memories. This is why we keep attracting the "perfect match" for our level of development. Once we let go of our memories, we let go of our programs, judgments, opinions, and expectations and then we can attract the right relationships at the right time.

I have news for you, the perfect relationship is the one that will show you what is in you that you need to let go!

Detaching and letting go of our memories works for every kind of relationship, even between parents and children. When we learn to let go, give without expectations, do what feels good in our hearts, and be ourselves, we free ourselves and others from the judgments, opinions and attachments that keep us from having healthy relationships. When we let go and detach, we discover peace and love within ourselves, and become more peaceful and loving towards others.

The first step is awareness. You must realize you are addicted to your attachments. Awareness is curative, and realizing you are not the addiction means immediate recognition that you are beyond all of this and it is only up to you to let go. Please know that addictions are also memories and can be erased. All you need to do is take 100% responsibility and let it go. You do not need to understand the why or how, just give God permission to erase the memories that no longer work for you.

Another way to engage in the process of letting go of your addiction to certain relationships or people in general, is to find replacements, something you enjoy, something that makes you feel good when you do it. Communing with nature is a good example. You can take walks in the park or on the beach. These types of activities help us to connect with our soul and allow us to let go and clean more easily. Engaging in activities you love for the activities themselves will help you to connect with the real you. Once you are in that place, letting go of what is not working in your life will just happen.

We have actually confused Love with what we think Love is (to be praised, approved of, accepted, cared for), but we do not feel fulfilled even when we obtain these things. Remember, the love you are looking for is just waiting for you, inside of you. True love for your self will open the doors to the love of the Universe.

****

Your interaction is requested about the chapter you just read...
Visit *http://www.hooponoponoway.com/theeasiestwaytolive/*
and ask any question you have or share your candid feedback.

Also find me on Facebook at: *www.Facebook.com/MabelKatz*

Mabel Katz
****

Chapter XXVI

Passion

Passion is our compass. If we trust and follow it, success is guaranteed. Unfortunately, what often happens is we go into a place of fear because trusting our passion is something foreign, uncertain, the unknown.

How many times have you been told that you are good at something and you should be doing it? I was personally told that I was good with numbers and should be an accountant. I went for it. It took me a long time to realize that this was not my heart's path. We always tend to do what gives us security because we don't enjoy uncertainty. But then we don't understand why we aren't motivated, or why we're not happy, even when we're making money.

Do you sometimes feel like you are on a treadmill, going nowhere? This feeling comes from denying your true identity. We think other people know better than us, so we do as they say. We usually go for the easier and less painful option, and unfortunately, we take a long time to realize that we can actually do what we love and enjoy it and still make money. How different the world would be if we followed our heart's true desire! When we feel fulfilled, we are better persons, and that affects our families, societies and the world at large.

Why are some people more successful than others? Perhaps some of them are doing what they love with a passion. Happy people create happy businesses, and people are more attracted to working in happy places. When we are happy, we are at peace, and if we are at peace, everybody else is too. Passionate people attract customers easily.

Our thoughts are so powerful that when we say we can, we can, and when we say we cannot, we cannot. But don't think you can control your mind and avoid negative memories. We actually don't have a clue of all the memories and programs playing sad songs in the background of our awareness. This is why simple schemes such as "Just think positive" don't usually work. The only way to clean our memories is to acknowledge that we have them, even if we don't know or understand what they are, and surrender them to the Source by giving the Universe permission to erase those that no longer serve us. See, the Universe is always waiting for us to take that first step. If you are willing to start trusting, miracles will happen.

When you follow your passion, nothing can go wrong, because you are following your heart. The heart is wise, and it has been patiently waiting for you to wake up. When you do what you love, money comes. Imagine making money doing something you wouldn't even think of charging for doing because you love it so much.

When you do what you love, you are in the flow. It is your natural path. Notice that being in the flow has nothing to do with thinking. When you are in the flow you are not thinking, you just move from inspiration. You are fully present, at point zero, devoid of judgments, expectations and preconceived ideas regarding how things should be. Check it out. People with money, don't work for their money. They love and enjoy what they do. They cannot call it work, and they are willing to do whatever it takes to practice what they love. They are in the flow. They are inspired.

When you allow Divinity to guide you, you find yourself in balance. You get perfect ideas and perfect relationships at the perfect time, because part of being successful is finding the right team to support you. Realize you are not perfect, and you don't have to be. You are unique. You were created to do something better than anybody else. It is important to know that others can do things that you can't. Working with these others will help you on your path. Once again, the right conditions, relationships and ideas will show up in your life when you realize you don't know anything and accept that God knows what is right and perfect for you. Your passion, enthusiasm, faith and humbleness will maintain you in the flow of life. This works for everybody. It doesn't matter if you have a university degree or not, if you have money or not. We all were born with a passion. We just need to remember what it is.

Know thyself. Find your true passion and follow it wherever it takes you. As soon as you realize that you have been asleep and become aware that it has been you all this time blocking yourself with thoughts of your own creation such as "There's not enough out there," "I don't deserve it," "I'm not good enough," you will automatically be in the flow and your negative programming will be unable to stop you. You will discover that, even though things might not have changed much on the "outside," you will be okay. You will be happy, free and at peace.

Trust and follow your heart and go for your passion! "To thine own self be true." - *William Shakespeare*

ଛ◆ଔ

 *Success*

Many times we get confused and tend to measure success with material possessions.

However, your chances of being happy and at peace are way higher if you realize that success has nothing to do with material things and that the success you are searching for is inside of you already. As a matter of fact, if you do not get in touch with your inner wealth and success, no amount of money will be enough to make you happy.

Success has to do with being YOU, happy and at peace, regardless of anything or anybody outside of yourself. Remember, everything you are looking for is inside yourself.

Real success comes from a source that does not change according to external circumstances. It is the result of knowing who you are and understanding the true nature of the Universe. Your wealth is your Identity. It is who you are, the talents you were born with, your ability to do things that nobody else can. It is your uniqueness. This type of clarity can bring you peace and much success.

When you are at zero, that is free of expectations, judgments and opinions, you realize you have everything and you don't need anything. Then you experience being in the flow and everything starts coming to you effortlessly.

There are many memories and programs running constantly in our conscious and subconscious mind telling us, for example, that it is not possible to succeed and make money doing what we love to do.

Passion should be your compass. Yes, I know, this takes TRUST, a lot of trust in the unknown.

You don't know for sure where you are heading, and trusting your heart can be scary, but the results are guaranteed.

Going for your dreams might take hard work, but the kind of work you cannot actually call work, because you love to do it. You would even pay to be able to do it. To succeed you must be persistent and know in your heart that you are willing to do whatever it takes to free yourself.

Remember, awareness is curative. We must strive to be conscious and become observers of life, without judgments and opinions. We can begin by noticing our thoughts, paying attention to our actions, and making sure we are present in the moment. It is very important to keep our old programming from running and controlling us, and the only way to do this is to re-record our programs.

We need to re-program ourselves, re-wire. Everything is a reflection of those old programs playing inside. Reality is not caused by others. We can let go of the programs that don't work for us anymore, even if we don't even know we have them.

We don't need to know which programs to delete or where they are stored. All we need to do is be willing to take 100% responsibility and simply let go.

What are you going to concentrate on and to whom are you going to pay attention? Will you listen to those who tell you it is not possible? Are you going to tell yourself it cannot be done and prove to the world that you are right by failing? Let me remind you that the outside voices you hear are not really outside and are simply reflections of the programs running inside. Are you willing to let go of those thoughts that don't serve you anymore? They brought you to where you are today, so thank them and let them go. You will find challenges on your way to self discovery, thank them, love them; they will help you go even further.

Sometimes you will need a little push, and God will bring you the right people to push you at the right time. Just let go instead of resisting those moments.

Letting go of old memories and programs replaying in your mind is essential if you want to be successful. Use the Ho'oponopono tools and clean. Say "Thank you" to your programs and give God permission to erase them. For example, you might have certain beliefs regarding what you need in order to be successful. Those beliefs are memories replaying. Some of them may be at a conscious level and some may be playing on very low volume (subconscious). You are not even aware you have these, but they talk to you all the time. Maybe you are already successful, but you do not know it because you are never satisfied and are always looking for and concentrating on what you don't have.

If you are willing to let go of your beliefs, you will be able to enjoy every step of the way and realize you are already successful because you are not a slave of your own opinions and judgments. Set yourself free and do what you love. You will attract success in an easier way.

ഌ ◆ ☊

 *Money*

If you want money, you need to let go of the victim mentality. You must cease blaming and be willing to take 100% responsibility. You must understand that you are in charge and everything is up to you. There is nobody out there. The victim mentally doesn't attract money; it attracts more poverty. We are so powerful, that if we just look to make ends meet, that is what we are going to attract. When we complain and blame, we attract more of what we do not want. Acting like a victim takes away our power.

Please realize wealth and money are not synonymous. We are wealthy regardless of whether we have money or not.

Having or not having money can't "make" you feel happy or unhappy. Money does not guarantee happiness. However, wealth will make you happy and peaceful. It is guaranteed, and fortunately, we are all born wealthy. Wealth is something you have inside and has nothing to do with possessions. It is your natural knowing, your natural talents, your identity. You were born with it.

Our beliefs about money, for example, play an enormously important role in our relationship with wealth. There are countless misinterpretations regarding the subject. For example, what do you think this means: "It is easier for a camel to go through the eye of a needle than for a rich man to enter the kingdom of God." -Mark 10.25

I am pretty sure it is not what you think it is. I actually asked my teacher Ihaleakalá, and he told me that what it really means is that you shouldn't put money first. You always want to put God and love first. Money will come when you do that. It is guaranteed.

Realizing the power of your thoughts about money is a MUST. If you think that having money is immoral, or that people who have money are greedy or did something illegal, money will elude you, because in your subconscious mind you think it is bad and thus you don't want it. There is nothing wrong with money. Wealthy people can go to heaven. Please do not worry. Go and make money, and always trust and do it God's (Love) way, not your way.

In reality, there is nothing wrong with having money, lots of money. As a matter of fact, you can make a difference if you have resources. In my case, God gives me more than I ever asked or dreamed of. I usually think that God has some plans for me which I do not know. And thanks to the resources He has granted me, I am able to make a difference in the lives of others, and I am grateful for this.

But let me tell you that first I had to put my heart on the line. I let go of my profitable career and then the resources came, not the other way around. The Universe is always watching and waiting for you to take that first step. It may feel scary, but when you do trust, amazing things come your way.

This may not be pleasant to consider, but if you don't have money, it's probably because you are afraid of it or you don't actually want it (subconsciously). You may believe somebody else has to take care of you, or you may simply be unwilling to do what it takes!

I've seen it happen before. People with money problems come to me asking for work, and no matter what suggestions I give them or what opportunities I point out, no matter what doors I open, they are always ready to say "No," no because of this, or no because of that. It is unbelievable!!

If you want money, say yes! There's always time to say "no" to opportunity. That may not seem like the route you want to take right now, but it is important to say YES. Why is this? Because when you say yes, you are opening doors, and you never know what or who could be there to offer you exactly what you are looking for.

Please stop blaming the economy or your parents!! YOU are the one turning away from the opportunities in front of you. Pay attention to how you invest your time. Complaining doesn't pay very good dividends.

Create something of value, a service or product that solves a problem or makes other people's lives easier. Usually we all feel really good by helping others, and when we create something of value, people usually go out of their way to give us business and recommend us to others.

People love to work with people that love what they do. You can tell. Don't you love it when people enjoy helping you, when they don't mind going the extra mile for you? Aren't you more willing to give them your money?

And remember, whatever you do, always do your best. Doors will open where you least expect, at the right time and the right place.

When you catch yourself blaming, criticizing, judging, CLEAN (let go)! Take action, trust, and especially let go of your pride. You do not need to know everything there is to know about a business before you start one. My teacher Ihaleakalá always says that he cannot imagine a God that would put us here and not give us what we need.

Let go of your poverty consciousness that tells you, "Maybe one day I will win the lottery." If you don't have money, at least take responsibility and say, "I choose not to have money at this time," and choose to be at peace without money.

And finally, remember. Not all of us come to this lifetime to make money. We all come here to learn and grow. On our path, we can have everything we need, and we can be happy and at peace with or without money.

When you let go, God will be able to work for you. He will guide you to the perfect goal. If you are with God, you have nothing to worry about.

Follow your passion and trust, and clean (let go) all the way. You will discover your wealth, and once you do, so much money will come that you will not know what to do with it!

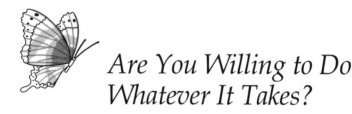

Are You Willing to Do Whatever It Takes?

You will answer YES, but for example, if you don't have money right now, it is because you are not doing what it takes. And believe me, I am not in any way suggesting that you engage in illegal, destructive, or dangerous activities.

Lately, I have been paying attention to and observing the attitudes of people around me who complain about lacking money. I am sorry for whatever is in me that has created the situation in which they don't have money. I take 100% responsibility for that, and I would like to share what I have noticed.

Sometimes it is hard to see the big picture and we are unwilling to do things that we don't like and enjoy. Neither are we willing to work longer hours or over the weekends. However, if you interview people that have "made it" or who simply have money, I am sure they will tell you they made some sacrifices to get there.

Let me go even further. The truth is, when you see the big picture, you don't even call it "sacrifice" because you don't judge the here and now. You have a clear idea of where you are going. The process might take lots of effort, perseverance, and discipline, but when you do what you love, you don't call it work, and much less a sacrifice. And even when you do what you love, you might have to do things that you love less, as part of the package, and you'll learn to love these things as well when you realize they will get you where you want to go.

We tend to have lots of opinions and judgments about everything. As a matter of fact, those who complain the most about their failures seem to be the first to criticize others. They think they understand exactly what other people should be doing and how. Little do they know that judging and criticizing are the main obstacles in their way.

A lot of us have the "manager" attitude. We might prefer not to work for others, or not to do something because "it's too hard." Listen, they say millionaires are made at midnight, when nobody sees their efforts, their commitment, or what they have to do to get there! Are you willing to work long hours? Work on weekends? Have less social life and end relationships that don't contribute anything to your life? You know what? Most of us aren't willing. However, I'm willing to bet that, if you ask people who have money, they will confirm that they worked very long hours and weekends included! So you see, you always choose, and you are free to choose whatever you want, but don't complain about the outcome, and stop judging.

We are often so fixated on what we don't want that, when we are offered an opportunity, we are not open enough to see the possibility, the exposure it would give us, or the people we would be able to meet. We are often unwilling to consider the steps we need to take to get where we want to go. In other words, we are not willing to do what it takes. It is painful to see, but we do it to ourselves. Nobody else is to blame. We have opinions and judgments and talk about others. We are experts on what others should be doing and saying and spend very little time looking at ourselves.

We must stop seeking the negative in every opportunity that presents itself, and stop the excuses and obstacles that we are so good at creating. This has nothing to do with positive thinking. The problem is that we are so close to the problem that we can't see the big picture and on top of that, we think we know it all!

We must give it everything we have.
You might say that you are working hard already, but that's not giving it everything you've got. Commitment is important. Having money means being "courageous," stretching beyond your comfort zones, and doing whatever it takes to get your heart's desires (not your intellect's desires). That means giving 100% of yourself, with no attitudes, and trusting in your heart that you are going to make it. It is all about doing what you

love with love, 100% responsibility, and 100% commitment.

Pay attention to where and what you are concentrating on. Be willing to make some sacrifices, maybe work hard, but most of all follow your heart, it knows better and can see the big picture, and it will help you get to the right place at the right time.

It may be hard to let go of judging and look at the big picture when we have been taught from childhood to dissect reality, analyze it and decide if it's good or bad. Fortunately, Ho'oponopono offers us excellent tools to change our lives without needing to do this. This ancient Hawaiian art of problem solving teaches that the part of us that knows better understands the big picture and is simply waiting for us to give it permission, so it can bring us the right opportunities.

Be willing to clean with the opportunities that come into your life. Be willing to be open. Stop fighting it and finding excuses or having your NOs always ready to fire. Please let go of your opinions and judgments and you will see how doors open where you least expect.

You might need to feel uncomfortable many times before the discomfort finally forces you to wake up, change your attitude, and achieve amazing results. But one day you will say enough is enough and you will be willing to let go of everything you thought you were. This may seem scary, as it is somewhat like dying. Your present false identity and sense of reality must die so you can become the real you. Imagine the tragedy; some people die without ever discovering who they really are!

Dare to experience life like a blind person does. Develop all your senses. Pay attention to the things that are important. See life through different eyes. If you do this, you'll experience existence in a completely different way, a way you didn't even know existed. Let go of what you think you know and play with life. Be willing to stretch. Feel the fear and do it anyway. But, most of all, be willing to do what it takes.

Bibliography

THE FOUNDATION OF I, INC. (Freedom Of the Cosmos) and IZI, LLC. Oahu, Hawaii. Tools, material and information used with permission, about the Hawaiian art of Ho'oponopono given through the seminars: *Self-Identity through Ho'oponopono*
www.self-i-dentity-through-hooponopono.com

Excerpts from *My Stroke of Insight: A Brain Scientist's Personal Journey*
By Jill Bolte Taylor, Ph.D | Copyright Jill Bolte Taylor, 2006
Trademark of My Stroke of Insight, Inc.

Excerpts from *The Way to Love: The Last Meditations of Anthony De Mello*
By Anthony De Mello | Published by Doubleday
Copyright 1991 by Gujarat Sahitya Prakash of Anand, India
Introduction copyright 1992 by J. Francis Stroud

Excerpts from *A Return To Love: Reflections on the Principles of A Course in Miracles* | By Marianne Williamson | First HarperPerennial edition published 1993. Reissued in 1996 | Copyright 1992 by Marianne Williamson

About the Author

Mabel Katz not only inspires change,
SHE will change your life forever!

Mabel Katz instills inspiration that will last a lifetime. With her inspirational approach, Mabel gives people the tools they need to change their lives and create lasting results. Her approach goes to people's core, their soul. Many have said she's changed their lives forever.

Mabel is internationally acclaimed as a foremost authority on the ancient Hawaiian art of **Ho'oponopono**. For twelve years she studied intensively with the master Ihaleakalá Hew Len, Ph.D. The essence of this art is simple, let go and let God. Who knows better than God what is right and perfect for us?

Author of ***The Easiest Way,*** based on Ho'oponopono and her business strategies for proven success. She just released a Special Edition of the book that started it all, *The Easiest Way,* now including this special bonus, ***The Easiest Way to Understanding Ho'oponopono,*** *The Clearest Answers to Your Most Frequently Asked Questions.* This Special Edition answers the what, where, when and why about cleaning. Cleaning is simply erasing your memories and bringing you back to Zero. She is also a contributing author to, ***Inspiration to Realization*** and ***Thank God I.***

Mabel's trainings have been attracting more parents to bring their children to learn the art of Ho'oponopono. This has delighted Mabel as she loves working with children. It also made Mabel realize that there was no age appropriate literature on Ho'oponopono for children. Mabel is elated to announce her first children's book *The Easiest Way to Grow.* This book is filled with beautiful illustrations that give the basics of Ho'oponopono in a fairy tale manner.

Zero Frequency is the book she is currently writing. This book was inspired by her realization that no matter what is going on around you if you are at zero (no judgments, no opinions, no expectations, or beliefs), you are open to allowing the goodness of God's universe to put you at the right time at the right place.

With her unmistakable style and grace, Mabel transcends languages. Her books have been translated and published into English, Spanish, Korean, Portuguese, Swedish, German, French, Russian, Hebrew and Romanian.

Born in Argentina, Mabel moved to Los Angeles in 1983 where she became a successful accountant, tax advisor, and Enrolled Agent. In 1997 Mabel started her own company, Your Business, Inc., a step that not only enhanced her own success but also increased her ability to work more directly with others. Her company had prospered by helping established businesses expand and grow.

A star in LA's Latino community, Mabel hosted the popular radio and television program, called "Despertar" (Awakening), and the "Mabel Katz Show" where she empowered Latinos by giving them the tools to start or grow a business, have fulfilled relationships and find financial success.

Ten years after starting her own business, Mabel decided to give up her successful accounting firm and talk show aspirations to follow just her passions. She is now on a journey that is taking her around the world as an author, seminar leader and speaker, inspiring many different cultures and languages.

As a result of her personal and business accomplishments and her generosity of spirit, Mabel has received acclaim on the local, national and now international level.

"Life is an inside job and it is much easier if we let it go and get out of our own way!"

—*Mabel Katz*

Telephone/Fax: (818) 668-2085 | support@mabelkatz.com
www.mabelkatz.com
www.hooponoponoway.com | www.zerofrequency.biz | www.businessbyyou.com

Ho'oponopono Resources from Mabel Katz

Mabel's book

http://www.mabelkatz.com/products_books.html
Discover more about Ho'oponopono and Mabel's personal journey in her book, ***The Easiest Way.***

Mabel's Ho'oponopono Q & A

http://mabelkatz.com/telewebcasts-monthly-q-and-a.htm
As you learn more about Ho'oponopono, you'll probably have more questions. Watch for announcements of Mabel's monthly Q & A TeleWebcasts. You can listen anywhere in the world and at any time.

Mabel's Ho'oponopono News

http://hooponoponoway.com
Sign up to receive Ho'oponopono tips, news, updates, and more. It's free.

Mabel's Blog, Forum, and News

http://hooponoponoway.com
Read Mabel's latest Ho'oponopono blog posts, articles, and
more. Share your story about Ho'oponopono, leave a comment,
ask a question on the forum.

Official Website of Mabel Katz

http://MabelKatz.com
Information about Mabel Katz, events' schedule, free audios,
videos and unique resources.

Your Business, Inc.

http://BusinessByYou.com
Discover Love, Wealth and Happiness with Ho'oponopono.
Mabel Katz and Dr. Ihaleakalá Hew Len can show you how.
Ho'oponopono events, videos, audios and tools, including
Ceeports®

Mabel's RSS News Feed

http://hooponoponoway.com/feed
Receive Mabel's blog news delivered to your email or favorite
RSS reader.

Mabel Katz Affiliate Program

http://MabelKatz.com/affiliates.htm
Sign up as an Affiliate and let us reward you for doing what
you're already doing, that is sharing with others about *The
Easiest Way.*

Follow Mabel on Twitter

http://twitter.com/MabelKatz
Read Mabel's latest Tweets on her Ho'oponopono journey.

Follow Mabel on Facebook

http://facebook.com/MabelKatzFanPage
Interact with Mabel on her Facebook page

Follow Mabel on Youtube

http://youtube.com/MabelKatz
Videos & Interviews with Mabel on her Youtube page.

Leave a voice/text testimonial

214-615-6505, ext. 9450 or *support@mabelkatz.com*
Mabel would love to hear your testimonial on how she has
touched your life.

How to Engage the Author

Mabel has become recognized in the field of personal effectiveness with her unique seminars for corporations and individuals. She takes her over 25 years of experience as an accountant and business leader and combines it with a simple formula. Based on the principles of Ho'oponopono, she teaches a system of applying practical principles for problem solving and achieving results; these seminars are particularly effective in accelerating self awareness, 100% responsibility, productivity and promoting accountability.

Mabel's seminars are on achieving abundance and fulfillment in a natural, easy way.

"We all have the power to change our lives without depending on anybody or anything outside ourselves."

—Mabel Katz

For more information on Mabel's workshops, seminars, speaking engagements or book orders you can contact the author at:

Your Business, Inc.

Your Business, Inc.
P.O. Box 427
Woodland Hills, CA 91365

Telephone/Fax: (818) 668-2085
support@mabelkatz.com
www.hooponoponoway.com
www.zerofrequency.biz
www.mabelkatz.com
www.businessbyyou.com

The Easiest Way to Live

*Let go of the past, live in the present and
change your life forever*

Table of Contents